101 *Blue-Ribbon* DESSERTS

Blue-Ribbon Pecan Pie, page 42

Julie's Strawberry Yum-Yum, page 83

Blueberry Pound Cake, page 10

Gooseberry Patch

An imprint of Globe Pequot
246 Goose Lane
Guilford, CT 06437

www.gooseberrypatch.com
1·800·854·6673

Copyright 2014, Gooseberry Patch 978-1-62093-158-5

Gooseberry Patch *cookbooks*

Aunt Marge's Peachy Pineapple Dessert, 79

Blueberry Cream Pie, 45

Since 1992, we've been publishing our own country cookbooks for every kitchen and for every meal of the day! Each title has hundreds of budget-friendly recipes, using ingredients you already have on hand in your pantry.

In addition, you'll find helpful tips and ideas on every page, along with our hand-drawn artwork and plenty of personality. Their lay-flat binding makes them so easy to use...they're sure to become a fast favorite in your kitchen.

Call us toll-free at
1·800·854·6673
and we'd be delighted to tell you all about our newest titles!

Shop with us online anytime at
www.gooseberrypatch.com

Find Gooseberry Patch wherever you are!
www.gooseberrypatch.com

Call us toll-free at 1·800·854·6673

Be a part of our bestselling cookbooks.

Share your tried & true recipes on our website and you'll be considered for our upcoming titles. If selected, your recipe will be printed along with your name and hometown. You'll even receive a FREE copy of the cookbook when it's published!

Frosty Butter Pecan Crunch Pie, page 53

Spiced Cranberry-Apple Crisp, page 84

Sour Cherry Lattice Pie, page 47

Cream Cheese Pound Cake, page 33

Golden Tequila Lime Tart, page 57

Country Rhubarb Crunch, page 76

Blue-Ribbon Pound Cake, page 35

CONTENTS

Piece of Cake 7

Easy as Pie........................... 40

Warm & Cozy........................74

Butterscotch Picnic Cake, page 12

Dedication

To everyone who's ever eaten their veggies just so they could get dessert.

Appreciation

To bakers everywhere who shared their prize-winning recipes... thank you!

Rustic Country Cherry Pie, page 59

Cherry Streusel Coffee Cake

Joyceann Dreibelbis
Wooster, OH

This easy-to-assemble recipe won Best of Show at our county fair several years ago, and no wonder. It's irresistible!

18-1/2 oz. pkg. yellow cake mix, divided
1 env. active dry yeast
1 c. all-purpose flour
2 eggs, beaten
2/3 c. warm water
5 T. butter, melted
21-oz. can cherry pie filling
2 T. sugar
Garnish: chopped nuts

Combine 1-1/2 cups dry cake mix, yeast, flour, eggs and warm water. Stir for 2 minutes; mix well. Spread in a greased 13"x9" baking pan. Blend melted butter and remaining cake mix; set aside. Spoon pie filling over batter in pan. Crumble butter mixture over pie filling. Sprinkle sugar over top. Bake at 375 degrees for 30 minutes; cool. Drizzle with glaze; sprinkle nuts on top. Serves 15.

Glaze:

1 c. powdered sugar
1 T. corn syrup
1 to 2 T. water

Combine powdered sugar and corn syrup. Stir in enough water to form a glaze consistency.

7

Prize-Winning Almond Bundt Cake

2-1/2 c. sugar
2 eggs, beaten
2-1/2 t. almond extract
1-1/3 c. milk
1 c. butter, softened
2-1/2 c. all-purpose flour
1 t. baking powder
1/4 t. cinnamon
Garnish: chopped almonds,
   raw sugar

In a bowl, beat together sugar, eggs, extract, milk and butter. Gradually add flour, baking powder and cinnamon; beat well. Sprinkle almonds and raw sugar in the bottom of a greased Bundt® pan; pour batter over almonds and sugar. Bake at 350 degrees for 50 minutes, or until a toothpick tests clean. Cool cake in pan for 15 to 20 minutes. Turn out onto a wire rack. Serve warm or cooled. Makes 12 servings.

Sarah Muennix
Flint, MI
I entered this Bundt cake into a baking contest at our local food store. It took home second place...and the bakery adopted this recipe to place alongside their other "gourmet" cakes!

Judy's Prize-Winning Toasted Pecan Cake

Judy Borecky
Escondido, CA

This local winner was featured on the front page of the San Diego newspaper!

2 c. chopped pecans
1-1/4 c. butter, softened and divided
3 c. all-purpose flour
2 t. baking powder
1/2 t. salt
2 c. sugar
4 eggs, beaten
1 c. milk
2 t. vanilla extract

Combine pecans and 1/4 cup butter; spread on a baking sheet. Bake at 350 degrees for 15 minutes, stirring often; cool. Mix flour, baking powder and salt. In a separate bowl, blend remaining butter and sugar; stir in eggs. Add flour mixture to butter mixture alternately with milk, beating well. Stir in vanilla and 1-1/3 cups pecans. Pour into 3 greased and floured 8" round cake pans. Bake at 350 degrees for 20 to 25 minutes, until cake tests done. Cool before frosting. Serves 12.

Frosting:

1/4 c. butter, softened
16-oz. pkg. powdered sugar
1 t. vanilla extract
4 to 6 T. evaporated milk
2/3 c. reserved toasted pecans

Beat all ingredients except pecans until smooth. Stir in pecans.

Blueberry Pound Cake

2-1/2 c. sugar
1/2 c. butter, softened
2 t. vanilla extract
8-oz. pkg. cream cheese,
   softened
4 eggs
2 c. fresh blueberries
3 c. all-purpose flour, divided
1 t. baking powder
1/2 t. baking soda
1/2 t. salt
8-oz. container lemon yogurt

Beat sugar, butter, vanilla and cream cheese with an electric mixer on medium speed until blended. Beat in eggs, one at a time. Toss blueberries with 2 tablespoons flour; set aside. Combine remaining flour, baking powder, baking soda and salt. Add flour mixture to sugar mixture alternately with yogurt. Fold in blueberries; pour into a greased tube pan. Bake at 350 degrees for one hour, or until a toothpick tests clean. Cool cake in pan for 10 minutes; turn out. Drizzle with Icing while still warm. Serves 16.

Icing:

1/2 c. powdered sugar
4 t. lemon juice

Combine ingredients to a drizzling consistency.

Suzy Grubich
Eighty Four, PA

I entered this cake in the county fair and won second place. A chocolate cake beat it out for the blue ribbon... it's tough to beat chocolate!

Tres Leches Cake

18-1/4 oz. pkg. yellow cake mix
14-oz. can sweetened condensed
  milk
5-oz. can evaporated milk
7.6-oz. can media crema, or 1 c.
  whole milk
8-oz. container frozen whipped
  topping, thawed
Optional: sliced strawberries,
  kiwi, pineapple, mandarin
  oranges

Prepare cake mix according to package instructions; bake in a 13"x9" baking pan. While cake is still warm, pierce surface all over with a skewer, every 1/2 inch. Combine milks; pour over cake slowly and evenly. Let cake stand at room temperature for 30 minutes. Cover with plastic wrap; refrigerate for at least 30 minutes, until well chilled. At serving time, frost cake with whipped topping; decorate with fruit, if desired. Keep refrigerated. Serves 8 to 10.

II

**Tina Butler
Royse City, TX**

This yummy Mexican-inspired cake is one of my favorites. Its name means "cake of three milks." The fruit topping looks so pretty, it's worth taking the time to do it.

Butterscotch Picnic Cake

1/2 c. butter
1 c. brown sugar, packed
3 eggs, beaten
1 t. vanilla extract
2 c. all-purpose flour
1 t. baking soda
1 t. salt
1-1/2 c. buttermilk
1 c. quick-cooking oats,
    uncooked
6-oz. pkg. butterscotch chips
1/3 c. chopped walnuts

Beat together butter and brown sugar
until light and fluffy. Blend in eggs
and vanilla; mix well. Whisk together
flour, baking soda and salt. Add flour
mixture to butter mixture alternately
with buttermilk, mixing well after
each addition. Stir in oats. Spread in a
greased 13"x9" baking pan. Combine
butterscotch chips and nuts; sprinkle
over top. Bake at 350 degrees for
30 to 35 minutes. Cool; cut into
squares. Serves 15 to 18.

Cindy Neel
Gooseberry Patch

This cake was in my
Grandmother Blanche's
collection of recipes that
she had gathered from
family & friends.

Debby's Orange Sherbet Cake

18-1/4 oz. pkg. orange supreme
  cake mix
6-oz. pkg. orange gelatin mix
16-oz. pkg. powdered sugar
2 6-oz. pkgs. frozen flaked
  coconut, thawed
8-oz. container sour cream
1 t. vanilla extract
2 T. frozen orange juice
  concentrate
12-oz. container frozen whipped
  topping, thawed
Garnish: 3-1/2 oz. can flaked
  coconut

Prepare cake mix according to
package directions. Add dry gelatin
mix; stir well. Spread batter in
3 greased and floured 9" round cake
pans. Bake at 350 degrees until
golden, 33 to 36 minutes. Cool
completely. For frosting, combine
powdered sugar, thawed coconut,
sour cream, vanilla and enough
orange juice to make a frosting
consistency. Set aside one cup
frosting. With a serrated knife, halve
each layer horizontally. Spread
remaining frosting between layers;
do not frost top of cake. Combine
reserved frosting and whipped
topping. Spread over top and sides of
cake; sprinkle with canned coconut.
Makes 18 servings.

Debby Conaway
Rome, GA

My most-requested cake
and also my mom's favorite.
It's so pretty...people are
amazed at the beautiful
color on the inside!

13

Oma's Lemon Cheesecake

**Cora Wilfinger
Manitowoc, WI**

A treasured recipe handed down from my grandmother. This wonderful treat has been present at every Christmas in my life...it is so worth the extra steps!

1-1/2 c. all-purpose flour
2-1/4 c. sugar, divided
1/2 c. butter, softened
4 eggs, divided
2 t. vanilla extract, divided
1 T. milk
1/2 t. salt
1 t. baking powder
2 8-oz. pkgs. cream cheese,
   softened
16-oz. container sour cream,
   divided
zest of 1 lemon, divided

Combine flour, 2/3 cup sugar, butter, 2 eggs, one teaspoon vanilla, milk, salt and baking powder. Mix well. Press evenly into the bottom and partially up the sides of a lightly greased 9" round springform pan. For filling, blend cream cheese with 1-1/2 cups sugar until smooth. Beat in remaining eggs, one at a time; stir in one cup sour cream, remaining vanilla and 2/3 of lemon zest. Pour filling into crust. Bake at 325 degrees for one hour. Turn off oven; leave pan in oven for 15 minutes. For topping, mix together remaining sour cream, sugar and zest until smooth. Spread topping over filling. Bake at 325 degrees for an additional 15 minutes. Cool before serving. Serves 12.

Strawberry Layer Cake

6-oz. pkg. strawberry gelatin mix
1/2 c. hot water
18-1/2 oz. pkg. white cake mix
2 T. all-purpose flour
1 c. strawberries, hulled and
    chopped
4 eggs

In a large bowl, dissolve dry gelatin mix in hot water; cool. Add dry cake mix, flour and strawberries; mix well. Add eggs, one at a time, beating slightly after each one. Pour batter into 3 greased 8" round cake pans. Bake at 350 degrees for 20 minutes, or until cake tests done with a toothpick. Cool; assemble layers with frosting. Serves 12.

Strawberry Frosting:

1/4 c. butter, softened
3-3/4 to 5 c. powdered sugar
1/3 c. strawberries, hulled and
    finely chopped

Blend butter and powdered sugar together, adding sugar to desired consistency. Add strawberries; blend thoroughly.

Steven Wilson
Chesterfield, VA

Growing up in North Carolina, spring meant strawberry time, when I'd go with Grandma to pick those luscious berries. She always baked this delicious cake for the Sunday night church social.

15

Blue-Ribbon Chocolate Cake

1/4 c. butter, softened
1/4 c. shortening
2 c. sugar
1 t. vanilla extract
2 eggs, beaten
1-3/4 c. all-purpose flour
3/4 c. baking cocoa
1/4 t. baking powder
3/4 t. salt
1-3/4 c. milk

Blend butter, shortening, sugar and vanilla until fluffy; blend in eggs and set aside. In a separate bowl, combine flour, cocoa, baking powder and salt; add flour mixture alternately with milk to sugar mixture. Stir well. Pour into 2 greased and floured 9" round cake pans. Bake at 350 degrees for 30 to 35 minutes, until a toothpick tests done. Cool and frost. Makes 16 servings.

Frosting:

6 T. butter, softened
1/2 c. baking cocoa
2-2/3 c. powdered sugar
1/3 c. milk
1 t. vanilla extract

To butter, add cocoa and powdered sugar alternately with milk. Mix in vanilla; stir until creamy.

Chris Leasure
Radnor, OH
A first-place winner in our county fair's baked goods division!

Bee Sting Cake

2 eggs, beaten
1 c. sugar
1 t. vanilla extract
1 c. all-purpose flour
1 t. baking powder
1/2 c. milk
2 T. butter

Beat together eggs, sugar, vanilla, flour and baking powder in a large bowl; set aside. Bring milk and butter to a boil in a saucepan over medium heat; mix well. Add to egg mixture; pour into a greased and floured 8"x8" baking pan. Bake at 350 degrees for 30 minutes, or until a toothpick tests done. Spread topping over warm cake. Broil until topping is bubbly and warm. Serves 10.

Topping:

10 T. brown sugar, packed
1/4 c. butter, melted
1/4 c. whipping cream
1 c. sweetened flaked coconut
1 t. vanilla extract

Combine all ingredients; mix well.

Jo Ann

This recipe is a shortcut version of an all-time favorite.

Fresh Apple Cake

1 c. oil
2 c. sugar
2 eggs, beaten
2-1/2 c. all-purpose flour
1 t. baking soda
1 t. salt
1 t. cinnamon
2 t. vanilla extract
3 c. Golden Delicious apples,
   cored and chopped
1 c. chopped pecans or walnuts
Optional: powdered sugar

Combine oil and sugar in a bowl; add
eggs and blend well. In a separate
bowl, mix flour, baking soda, salt
and cinnamon; add to oil mixture
and blend well. Stir in vanilla, apples
and nuts. Batter will be very stiff.
Spoon into a greased and floured
tube pan. Bake at 350 degrees for
50 to 60 minutes. Turn out cake.
Sprinkle with powdered sugar, if
desired. Serves 16 to 20.

Gail Allen
Brownfield, TX

This recipe came from my
mother years ago...she was
the best cook. I have made
this cake for many years and
in 1978 won a blue ribbon and
Best in Category at the fair.

Banana-Nut Cake

Connie Garcia
Hobbs, NM

This recipe is over 100 years old. Mom got it from her Sunday School teacher. When I entered this cake at the Lovington, New Mexico fair, I won a blue ribbon!

3 egg whites
1 c. sugar
1/2 c. butter, melted
2 egg yolks
1-1/2 c. buttermilk
1 t. baking soda
3 c. all-purpose flour
2 t. baking powder
3 ripe bananas, mashed
1 t. vanilla extract
1 c. chopped walnuts
Garnish: cream cheese frosting

Beat egg whites until frothy; set aside. In a large separate bowl, beat together all ingredients except garnish, adding egg whites last. Divide batter among 3 greased and floured 9" round cake pans. Bake at 350 degrees for 30 minutes, or until cake tests done. Cool; assemble cake with frosting. Serves 12 to 15.

19

Kay's Carrot Cake

20-oz. can crushed pineapple
3 eggs, beaten
3/4 c. oil
1 t. vanilla extract
2 c. brown sugar, packed
2 c. carrots, peeled and grated
1 c. flaked coconut
3 c. all-purpose flour
3-1/8 t. baking powder
1 t. baking soda
1 t. salt
2 t. cinnamon
3/4 c. toasted walnuts, chopped

Purée pineapple with juice; set aside.
In a bowl, beat eggs, oil and vanilla.
In a large saucepan over low heat, stir
egg mixture into brown sugar. Cook
just until caramelized; stir in carrots,
coconut and pineapple. Mix
remaining ingredients except walnuts;
add to carrot mixture a little at a time.
Stir just until moistened. Toss walnuts
with a little flour; fold into batter.
Pour into a greased 13"x9" baking pan.
Bake at 375 degrees for 10 minutes.
Reduce heat to 325 degrees; bake for
45 minutes. Cool; frost. Serves 18.

Cream Cheese Icing:

1/4 c. butter, softened
8-oz. pkg. cream cheese, softened
6-1/2 c. powdered sugar

Beat butter with cream cheese.
Gradually beat in powdered sugar.

Karen Gee
Carlingford, New
Brunswick

I entered a baking contest
with this recipe and won
first place...this cake is
truly a winner!

Peach Cobbler Muffins

3 c. all-purpose flour
1 c. sugar
1-1/2 T. baking soda
1/2 t. salt
3/4 c. butter, diced
1-3/4 c. milk
15-oz. can sliced peaches,
    drained and chopped

Mix flour, sugar, baking soda and
salt in a large bowl. Cut in butter
with a pastry blender or a fork. Add
milk and peaches; stir just until
moistened. Spoon batter into
18 greased muffin cups, filling
2/3 full. Spoon topping onto
muffins. Bake at 400 degrees for
18 to 20 minutes, until golden.
Turn out and cool slightly on a
wire rack; serve warm or cooled.
Makes 1-1/2 dozen.

Topping:

2 T. butter, diced
2 T. sugar
1/2 t. cinnamon

Mix together in a small bowl until
crumbly.

Bonnie Allard
Santa Rosa, CA

My most-requested muffins...
my family & friends love
them! They disappear right
away whenever I make them
to share.

21

Cherry Loaf Cake

2 c. sugar
2 c. all-purpose flour
2 T. margarine, melted
2 eggs, beaten
2 t. baking soda
2 T. water
15-oz. can tart or sweet cherries
1 c. chopped walnuts
Garnish: whipped cream

In a bowl, mix together sugar, flour, margarine, eggs and baking soda dissolved in water. Add cherries with juice; stir in nuts, mixing well. Spread batter in a greased 13"x9" baking pan. Bake at 375 degrees for 30 minutes. Pierce top of warm cake with a fork. Pour hot topping over cake; cool. Serve with whipped cream. Flavor is best 2 to 3 days after baking. Serves 12 to 15.

Topping:

2 c. brown sugar, packed
2 T. all-purpose flour
2 c. hot water
2 t. vanilla extract

Combine all ingredients in a saucepan over medium heat; bring to a boil.

Wanda Simon
Hutchinson, KS

This is a prize-winning cake I entered in our local newspaper's recipe contest. It's a very old recipe, a rich cake that keeps up to 10 days in the refrigerator.

Red Velvet Cake

2-1/2 c. all-purpose flour
1-1/2 c. sugar
1 t. salt
1 t. baking cocoa
1 c. buttermilk
1-1/2 c. oil
2 eggs, beaten
1 t. vanilla extract
1-oz. bottle red food coloring
1 t. white vinegar
1 t. baking soda

In a large bowl, mix flour, sugar, salt and cocoa. Add buttermilk, oil, eggs and vanilla; mix well. Stir in food coloring. Mix vinegar and baking soda; add to batter and stir just until well blended. Pour into 3 greased and floured 9" round cake pans. Bake at 325 degrees for 30 to 35 minutes, until a toothpick tests clean. Cool; assemble with frosting. Serves 10 to 12.

Cream Cheese Frosting:

8-oz. pkg. cream cheese, softened
1/2 c. butter, softened
1 t. vanilla extract
6 c. powdered sugar
Optional: chopped pecans

Blend cream cheese, butter and vanilla. Stir in powdered sugar until smooth; add nuts, if using.

23

Peggy Frazier
Indianapolis, IN

When my daughter Julie was young, I helped her make this cake for a fundraiser. She won first prize and still has the blue ribbon!

County Fair Grand Champion Cake

2 c. all-purpose flour
2 t. baking soda
1/4 t. salt
3 1-oz. sqs. semi-sweet baking
    chocolate
1 c. oil, divided
2 15-oz. cans sliced beets,
    drained
1-3/4 c. sugar
3 eggs, beaten
1 t. vanilla extract
Garnish: baking cocoa,
    powdered sugar

Mix together flour, baking soda and salt; set aside. Melt chocolate with 1/4 cup oil in a double boiler; set aside. Purée beets in a blender; measure 2 cups and set aside. Blend sugar and eggs in a large bowl; gradually mix in remaining oil, pureéd beets, melted chocolate and vanilla. Stir in flour mixture; mix well. Grease a Bundt® pan and dust with cocoa; pour batter into pan. Bake at 375 degrees for one hour, or until a toothpick tests clean. Cool for 15 minutes on a wire rack. Turn out cake; dust with powdered sugar. Makes 10 to 12 servings.

Cindy Conway
Elizabeth, CO
You'll never believe the surprise ingredient that makes this cake a winner... it's beets!

Pineapple Sheet Cake

2 c. all-purpose flour
2 c. sugar
2 t. baking soda
1 t. vanilla extract
2 eggs, beaten
20-oz. can crushed pineapple
Optional: chopped pecans

In a large bowl, combine flour, sugar, baking soda, vanilla, eggs and undrained pineapple. Mix well. Spread batter in a greased and floured 15"x10" jelly-roll pan. Bake at 325 degrees for 30 minutes, until cake tests done with a toothpick. Spread with frosting while still warm. Sprinkle with pecans, if desired. Cool; cut into squares. Makes 15 servings.

Cream Cheese Frosting:

8-oz. pkg. cream cheese, softened
1/2 c. butter, softened
1 t. vanilla extract
1 c. powdered sugar

In a large bowl, blend all ingredients together until smooth.

25

Teresa Moore
Pawhuska, OK
I first tasted this cake at a church supper. It was so good, I went back for seconds! Try it and you'll agree.

Grandma's Cherry Pudding Cake

1/4 c. butter, softened
2 c. sugar, divided
2 c. all-purpose flour
4 t. baking powder
1 c. milk
1 c. hot water
2 c. sour cherries, pitted
Optional: vanilla ice cream

In a bowl, blend butter and one cup sugar; set aside. In a separate bowl, mix flour and baking powder. Add flour mixture and milk alternately to butter mixture. Stir until smooth; turn into a greased 8"x8" baking pan. In another bowl, mix remaining sugar, hot water and cherries. Pour over batter in pan; do not stir. Bake at 350 degrees for 40 minutes. Carefully remove pan from oven. Dessert will be thin on the bottom, with cherries and cake on top. As it cools, bottom layer will thicken into a sauce. Serve warm, scooping out cake and spooning some sauce over top. Garnish with a scoop of ice cream, if desired. Serves 9.

Linda Basham
Gardner, IL

Grandma made this cake every summer with fresh cherries from our trees. I still enjoy picking the cherries to make this dessert.

Pecan Pie Muffins

1 c. chopped pecans
1 c. brown sugar, packed
1/2 c. all-purpose flour
2 eggs
1/2 c. butter or coconut oil,
   melted and cooled slightly

Mix pecans, brown sugar and flour
in a large bowl; make a well in the
center and set aside. In a separate
bowl, beat eggs just until foamy; stir
in butter or oil. Add pecan mixture
to egg mixture; stir just until
moistened. Spoon batter into
9 muffin cups greased only on the
bottom, filling 2/3 full. Bake at
350 degrees for 20 to 25 minutes,
until golden. Promptly remove
muffins from muffin tin; cool on
a wire rack. Makes 9 muffins.

27

Melynda Hoffman
Fort Wayne, IN

When my daughter Brooke took
these scrumptious muffins to
the Allen County Fair, she
won a blue ribbon. All the
judges asked for another
muffin...please!

Blue-Ribbon Pumpkin Roll

2/3 c. canned pumpkin
3 eggs, beaten
1 c. sugar
3/4 c. all-purpose flour
1 t. baking soda
1 t. cinnamon
1 c. plus 3 T. powdered sugar,
    divided
8-oz. pkg. cream cheese,
    softened
1 t. vanilla extract

Blend together pumpkin, eggs and sugar. In a separate bowl, combine flour, baking soda and cinnamon; fold into pumpkin mixture. Line a 15"x10" jelly-roll pan with parchment paper. Grease and flour the paper; spread batter into pan. Bake at 350 degrees for 15 minutes. Sprinkle 3 tablespoons powdered sugar on a tea towel; turn out warm cake onto towel. Carefully peel off parchment paper. Starting at narrow end, roll up cake and towel together; cool completely on a wire rack, seam-side down. Blend cream cheese, remaining powdered sugar and vanilla until smooth. Unroll cake; spread with cream cheese mixture and re-roll, removing towel as you roll. Place on a serving plate, seam-side down; cover and chill at least 2 hours. Serves 10 to 12.

Laurie Ellithorpe
Argyle, NY

This yummy recipe is blue-ribbon good and party perfect!

Dad's Apple Cake

4 c. McIntosh apples, peeled,
   cored and cubed
2 c. sugar
1 c. oil
2 t. cinnamon
2 t. vanilla extract
1/2 t. salt
1 c. raisins
1-1/2 c. hot water
3 eggs, beaten
3 c. all-purpose flour
2 t. baking soda
1 c. chopped walnuts
Garnish: whipped cream

In a large bowl, mix together apples, sugar, oil, cinnamon, vanilla and salt. Let stand for one hour. In a small bowl, cover raisins with hot water; let stand for 10 minutes and drain well. Add raisins to apple mixture along with remaining ingredients except garnish. Stir well; pour into a greased 13"x9" baking pan. Bake at 350 degrees for 45 minutes, or until a toothpick inserted in the center tests clean. Cut into squares; garnish with whipped cream. Serves 12 to 15.

29

Sally Hines
Old Forge, PA

This cake was a favorite of my father-in-law. He visited us every Sunday, and in fall he brought us apples from the local orchard. This won me a prize from my local newspaper!

Summer Lemon Cake

18-1/2 oz. pkg. lemon cake mix
4 eggs
3/4 c. water
3/4 c. oil
3.4-oz. pkg. instant lemon
    pudding mix

Prepare cake as directed on package, adding dry pudding mix to batter. Pour batter into a greased 13"x9" baking pan. Bake at 350 degrees for 28 to 33 minutes, until cake tests done with a toothpick. Poke holes in hot cake with a fork. Pour glaze over cake. Cool before cutting. Serves 12 to 15.

Frosting Glaze:

2 c. powdered sugar
1/4 c. lemon juice
1/4 c. oil
1/4 c. hot water

Combine powdered sugar, lemon juice and oil in a bowl. Stir together, adding enough hot water to form a glaze consistency.

Brenda Huey
Geneva, IN

This is a very moist cake and so refreshing in hot weather.

Strawberry Shortcake Cake

1 c. all-purpose flour
1/2 c. sugar
2 t. baking powder
1/8 t. salt
1 egg, lightly beaten
1/2 c. milk
1/2 t. vanilla extract
2 T. butter, melted
1-1/2 c. strawberries, hulled
   and sliced

In a bowl, combine flour, sugar, baking powder, and salt. In a separate bowl, combine egg, milk, vanilla and butter. Add egg mixture to flour mixture; stir well. Spread batter in a greased 8"x8" baking pan. Top with berries; sprinkle with topping. Bake at 375 degrees for 35 minutes, or until cake tests done. Serves 8.

Topping:
1/2 c. all-purpose flour
1/2 c. sugar
1/4 c. butter, softened
Optional: 1/4 c. chopped walnuts

Mix together in a small bowl.

31

Julie Kovach
Brunswick, OH
I found this recipe 20 years ago and it has become a family favorite. I even won a blue ribbon with it at our local carnival.

Fruit Cocktail Cake

2 eggs
1-1/2 c. sugar
2 t. baking soda
1/2 t. salt
15-oz. can fruit cocktail
2 c. all-purpose flour
Garnish: whipped cream

Beat eggs. Add sugar, baking soda, salt and fruit cocktail with juice; mix well. Add flour; mix well again. Pour batter into a greased 13"x9" baking pan. Bake at 350 degrees for 45 minutes, or until cake tests done. While still hot, pour warm sauce over cake; let stand until absorbed. Serve warm with whipped cream. Keeps for several days if refrigerated. Serves 12.

Butter Sauce:

3/4 c. sugar
1/2 c. milk
1/2 c. butter
1 t. vanilla extract

Combine sugar, milk and butter in a small saucepan; bring to a boil over medium-low heat. Remove from heat; stir in vanilla.

Janis Parr
Campbellford, Ontario
This special cake is very moist and flavorful, with a warm sauce over top. It's very easy to make and always a hit.

Cream Cheese Pound Cake

1 c. all-purpose flour
18-1/2 oz. pkg. yellow butter
  cake mix
1/2 c. butter, softened
1 c. sugar
4 eggs
8-oz. pkg. cream cheese,
  softened
1/2 t. vanilla extract
1 c. milk

Combine flour and dry cake mix in a bowl; set aside. In a separate bowl, blend together butter and sugar until very creamy. Add eggs, one at a time, mixing well; add cream cheese and vanilla. Alternately add flour mixture and milk to butter mixture, starting and ending with flour mixture. Pour batter into a greased and floured tube pan. Place pan in a cold oven; turn oven to 325 degrees. Bake for one hour, or until cake tests done with a toothpick. Serves 12 to 14.

33

Wanda Pardue Foster
Wilkesboro, NC

This cake won two blue ribbons for me at the county fair! I like to blend the butter and sugar with my hands...it results in a better cake.

Holiday Orange Cake

1/2 c. buttermilk
1 t. baking soda
1 c. butter, softened
2 c. sugar
4 eggs
3-1/2 c. all-purpose flour
1/4 t. salt
2 T. orange juice
8-oz. pkg. chopped dates
2 c. chopped pecans
1 lb. orange slice candy, chopped
1 c. flaked coconut

Combine buttermilk and baking soda; set aside. Blend butter and sugar; beat in eggs, one at a time. Combine flour and salt; add to butter mixture alternately with buttermilk. Fold in remaining ingredients; pour into a well-floured tube pan. Bake at 250 degrees for 2 hours. Pour glaze over hot cake while still in pan. Cool; turn out of pan. Serves 12.

Glaze:

2 c. powdered sugar
1 c. orange juice

Stir together ingredients until smooth.

Naomi Townsend
Ozark, MO

This fruitcake was always our holiday favorite. Mother baked this cake for the county fair in July and always took home a blue ribbon!

Blue-Ribbon Pound Cake

1 c. butter, softened
1/2 c. shortening
3 c. sugar
6 eggs
3-1/2 c. self-rising flour
1/2 t. baking powder
1/8 t. salt
1 c. milk
2 t. lemon extract
zest and juice of 1 lemon

In a bowl, blend butter and shortening; stir in sugar. Add eggs, one at a time. Add flour, baking powder, salt and milk; mix well. Stir in lemon extract, zest and juice; mix well and pour into a greased and floured Bundt® pan. Bake at 325 degrees for 2 hours, or until cake tests done. Turn onto a cake plate; let cool. Makes 12 to 15 servings.

35

Crystal Shook
Catawba, NC

I made this pound cake for a reunion and won a first-place blue ribbon!

Nutmeg Feather Cake

1/4 c. butter, softened
1/4 c. shortening
1-1/2 c. sugar
3 eggs, beaten
2 c. all-purpose flour
1/4 t. salt
1 t. baking powder
1 t. baking soda
2 t. nutmeg
1 c. buttermilk
1/2 t. vanilla extract

Blend together butter, shortening and sugar. Add eggs; beat well. In a separate bowl, whisk together flour, salt, baking powder, baking soda and nutmeg; set aside. In a small bowl, combine buttermilk and vanilla. Add flour mixture to shortening mixture alternately with buttermilk mixture. Spread in a greased, parchment paper-lined 13"x9" baking pan. Bake at 350 degrees for 25 to 30 minutes, until cake is golden and tests done. Serves 8 to 10.

Faye Mayberry
Saint David, AZ
This recipe was discovered in a vintage cookbook dated 1952 and it's a keeper. We top warm servings with a pat of butter...heavenly!

Tried & True Bundt Cake

1-1/2 c. butter, softened
8-oz. pkg. cream cheese,
    softened
3 c. sugar
6 eggs
3 c. all-purpose flour
1/8 t. salt
1 T. vanilla extract
Optional: powdered sugar or
    powdered sugar glaze

In a bowl, beat butter and cream
cheese with an electric mixer on
medium speed until creamy.
Gradually add sugar, beating well.
Beat in eggs, one at a time. In a
separate bowl, combine flour and
salt; beat in gradually on low speed
just until blended. Stir in vanilla.
Pour batter into a greased and
floured 10" Bundt® pan. Bake at
300 degrees for one hour and
40 minutes, or until a toothpick tests
clean. Cool cake in pan on a wire
rack 10 to 15 minutes. Turn out of
pan onto rack; cool completely.
If desired, sprinkle with powdered
sugar or drizzle with powdered sugar
glaze. Serves 15.

37

Elizabeth Cisneros
Eastvale, CA
This recipe never fails...
it has won blue ribbons
at the county fair
several times!

Mocha Pudding Cake

1 c. all-purpose flour
1 c. sugar, divided
6 T. baking cocoa, divided
1-1/2 t. baking powder
1/4 t. salt
1/2 c. milk
3 T. oil
1 t. vanilla extract
1/2 c. mini semi-sweet
   chocolate chips
1 c. strong brewed coffee
Garnish: vanilla ice cream or
   whipped cream

Combine flour, 2/3 cup sugar, 4 tablespoons cocoa, baking powder and salt in a large bowl. In a separate bowl, stir together milk, oil and vanilla. Add to flour mixture; stir just until blended. Spread batter in a lightly greased 8"x8" baking pan. Combine chocolate chips with remaining sugar and cocoa; sprinkle evenly over batter. Bring coffee to a boil and pour evenly over batter; do not stir. Bake at 350 degrees for 25 to 30 minutes, until cake springs back when lightly pressed in center. Garnish as desired. Serves 8 to 10.

Lanita Anderson
Chesapeake, VA
This delicious recipe was given to me by a fellow chaplain's wife. Even guests who don't usually care for coffee love this cake!

Gram's Rhubarb Coffee Cake

1/2 c. butter, softened
1-1/2 c. brown sugar, packed
1 egg, beaten
2 c. all-purpose flour
1/2 t. baking soda
1/2 t. salt
1 c. buttermilk
1-1/2 t. vanilla extract
1-1/2 c. rhubarb, chopped
1/3 c. sugar
1 T. cinnamon

In a bowl, blend together butter and brown sugar; stir in egg. In a separate bowl, mix flour, baking soda and salt. Add flour mixture to butter mixture alternately with buttermilk and vanilla. Stir in rhubarb. Pour batter into a greased 9"x9" baking pan; sprinkle with sugar and cinnamon. Bake at 350 degrees for 40 minutes. Serve warm. Serves 9.

39

Judy Marsh
Allentown, PA
This was Grandma Leona's original recipe which won 2nd place in the 1970 Pillsbury Bake-Off Contest. It's been a winner in our family forever!

Apple Hand Pies

2 Granny Smith apples, peeled,
  cored and diced
1/3 c. sugar
1/2 t. cinnamon
2 c. all-purpose flour
1 t. salt
1/2 c. shortening
1/2 c. cold water
1 c. oil
Garnish: coarse sugar

Mix apples, sugar and cinnamon in a saucepan over low heat Cook for 8 to 10 minutes, until apples are tender. Set aside. Combine flour and salt; cut in shortening with a fork. Stir in water to a dough consistency. Roll out dough 1/8-inch thick on a floured surface. Cut out with a 4-inch round cookie cutter; place one tablespoon apple mixture in center of each circle. Sprinkle edges with water; fold circles in half. Seal edges with a fork; set aside. Heat oil in a skillet over medium-high heat. Fry pies, a few at a time, for 2 to 3 minutes per side, until golden. Drain on paper towels; sprinkle with coarse sugar while still warm. Makes 6 to 8 pies.

Rita Morgan
Pueblo, CO
These taste just like the fried pies at the county fair!

Peach Melba Pie

4 peaches, peeled, pitted
  and sliced
1 c. sugar
5 t. lemon juice
1/4 c. cornstarch
1/3 c. water
3 c. fresh raspberries
9-inch pie crust, baked

In a large saucepan over medium heat, combine peaches, sugar and lemon juice. In a small bowl, stir cornstarch and water until smooth; stir into peach mixture. Bring to a boil; cook and stir one minute, or until thickened. Remove from heat; cool to room temperature. Gently fold in raspberries; spoon into baked pie crust. Chill at least 3 hours to overnight. Serves 6.

41

Barb Lueck
Lester Prairie, MN
I got this recipe from my mom. It is our favorite summer pie. Although we can't grow peaches in Minnesota, we have an abundance of raspberries!

Blue-Ribbon Pecan Pie

9-inch pie crust, unbaked
1/2 c. pecan halves
3 eggs
1 c. dark corn syrup
1 c. sugar
1 t. vanilla extract
1/8 t. salt

Place unbaked crust in a 9" pie plate. Arrange pecans in crust; set aside. In a bowl, beat eggs well. Add remaining ingredients; mix well. Pour mixture over pecans in crust. Bake at 400 degrees for 15 minutes; reduce oven to 325 degrees. Bake an additional 30 minutes, or until center of pie is set. Cool completely. Serves 8.

Gail Kelsey
Phoenix, AZ

This pie has won a blue ribbon at our state fair every time I entered it! It's a family favorite and is always a part of our Christmas dinner.

Caramel Apple Pie

36 to 40 caramels, unwrapped
2 T. water
6 c. Granny Smith and/or
    Golden Delicious apples,
    peeled, cored and sliced
1 T. lemon juice
9-inch pie crust, unbaked
3/4 c. all-purpose flour
3 T. brown sugar, packed
1/2 t. cinnamon
1/2 t. nutmeg
1/4 t. salt
6 T. butter
1/2 c. chopped pecans

Combine caramels and water in the
top of a double boiler. Cook and stir
over low heat until caramels melt.
Sprinkle apples with lemon juice.
Layer apples in unbaked pie crust
alternately with layers of melted
caramel. In a separate bowl,
combine flour, brown sugar, spices
and salt. Cut in butter with a pastry
blender; stir in pecans. Sprinkle
mixture evenly over apples. Bake at
375 degrees for 40 minutes, or until
golden and apples are tender.
Serves 8.

Joie Cunningham
Wrightstown, WI
I entered this recipe in a
contest for a local TV
cooking show...and won!
I make it for the holidays
and my daughter Rachael
loves to help me.

43

Banana Pudding Pie

4 c. milk
2 3-oz. pkgs. cook & serve
   banana pudding mix
1 to 2 ripe bananas, sliced
   and divided
9-inch pie crust, baked
1 c. whipping cream
1/4 c. powdered sugar
1/4 t. banana extract

Bring milk to a boil in a saucepan
over medium-high heat. Reduce heat
to medium. Add dry pudding mixes;
whisk constantly until thickened.
Remove from heat; cover and chill
for 4 hours. Once pudding is cool,
arrange bananas in bottom of baked
pie crust, reserving a few slices for
garnish. Spoon pudding over
bananas. With an electric mixer on
high speed, beat cream until soft
peaks form. Beat in powdered sugar
and extract, starting on medium
speed and increasing to high, until
stiff peaks form. Spoon whipped
cream over pie, or spoon into a
piping bag and pipe onto pie.
Garnish with reserved banana slices;
chill. Serves 8 to 10.

Kathy Collins
Brookfield, CT

I found this recipe while
I was searching through all
the recipes my mother had
clipped out. I made it for
my family one night, and
it's now a keeper!

Blueberry Cream Pie

8-oz. container sour cream
2 T. all-purpose flour
3/4 c. sugar
1 t. vanilla extract
1/4 t. salt
1 egg, beaten
2-1/2 c. fresh blueberries
9-inch pie crust, unbaked

In a bowl, combine all ingredients except blueberries and crust. Beat with an electric mixer on high speed until well mixed, about 2 minutes. Fold in blueberries; pour into unbaked pie crust. Bake at 400 degrees for 25 minutes; remove from oven. Sprinkle pie with topping; bake an additional 10 minutes. Chill before serving. Serves 6 to 8.

Topping:
3 T. all-purpose flour
1 T. sugar
1-1/2 t. butter
3 T. chopped pecans or walnuts

Stir ingredients together until crumbly.

45

Carol Patterson
Deltona, FL

This delectable pie won me a blue ribbon at the county fair!

Tennessee Fudge Pie

2 eggs
1/2 c. butter, melted and cooled
   slightly
1/4 c. baking cocoa
1/4 c. all-purpose flour
1 c. sugar
2 t. vanilla extract
1/3 c. semi-sweet chocolate chips
1/3 c. chopped pecans
9-inch pie crust, unbaked
Garnish: whipped cream,
   chocolate curls

In a bowl, beat eggs slightly; stir in melted butter. Add remaining ingredients except crust; mix well and pour into crust. Bake at 350 degrees for about 25 minutes, until firm. Cool before slicing; garnish as desired. Makes 8 servings.

Dusty Cannon
Paxton, IL

Mama has always made this pie for our Thanksgiving. People request it for church socials and parties too...it's a chocolate lover's dream!

Sour Cherry Lattice Pie

2 9-inch pie crusts, unbaked
4 c. sour cherries, pitted and
    1/2 c. juice reserved
1 c. sugar
1 T. all-purpose flour
2-1/2 T. cornstarch
juice and zest of one lime
2 T. butter, diced
1 egg, beaten
2 T. whipping cream

Place one crust in a 9" pie plate. Wrap with plastic wrap; chill. Cut remaining crust into one-inch wide strips; cut leftover crust into star shapes with a cookie cutter. Place lattice strips and stars on a parchment paper-lined baking sheet; cover with plastic wrap and chill. Combine cherries and juice in a large bowl. Sprinkle with sugar, flour, cornstarch, lime juice and zest. Toss well and pour into pie crust; dot with butter. Weave lattice strips over filling. Arrange stars on lattice. Whisk together egg and cream; brush over crust. Bake at 400 degrees for about 50 minutes, until bubbly and crust is golden. Cool slightly before cutting. Serves 6 to 8.

47

Sharon Demers
Dolores, CO

When I was little, my father would sing, "Can you bake a cherry pie, Sharon girl, Sharon girl?" and I would giggle and say "Nooo!" Well, now I can!

Skillet Cherry Pie

1/4 c. butter
1/2 c. brown sugar, packed
2 9-inch frozen pie crusts,
    unbaked
15-oz. can tart cherries, drained
21-oz. can cherry pie filling
1/4 c. sugar
1 T. plus 1/8 t. all-purpose flour
1 to 2 T. milk
Garnish: powdered sugar

In a cast-iron skillet, melt butter with brown sugar over medium-low heat. Remove from heat. Place one frozen pie crust in skillet on top of butter mixture; set aside. In a bowl, mix cherries and pie filling; spoon into crust. Mix sugar and flour together in a cup; sprinkle evenly over cherry mixture. Place remaining frozen pie crust upside-down on top of cherry mixture. Brush with milk; cut slits in crust to vent. Bake at 350 degrees for one hour, or until bubbly and crust is golden. Cool; sprinkle with powdered sugar. Serves 8.

Pearl Teiserskas
Brookfield, IL
I used to make this quick cherry pie to take to our church socials. It literally takes five minutes to prepare and is oh-so good!

$165 Blackberry-Apple Pie

2 9-inch pie crusts, unbaked
2-1/2 lbs. Gala apples, peeled,
    cored and sliced
2 c. frozen blackberries
1 c. sugar
2 T. all-purpose flour
1 to 2 t. cinnamon
1/2 t. nutmeg
1 T. butter, diced
Garnish: additional sugar and
    cinnamon
Optional: vanilla ice cream

Place one pie crust in a 9" pie plate;
set aside. In a bowl, combine apples,
blackberries, sugar, flour and spices.
Toss to mix; spoon into crust. Dot
pie with butter; top with remaining
crust. Pinch edges to seal and cut
vents; decorate with crust cut-outs,
if desired. Sprinkle with additional
sugar and cinnamon. Bake at
375 degrees for one to 1-1/2 hours,
until fruit is bubbly and top crust is
golden. Serve topped with ice cream,
if desired. Makes 6 to 8 servings.

49

Marian Forck
Chamois, MO

My husband Bernie makes
this every year for the
Frankenstein, MO Fall Supper
pie auction. One year it went
for 165 dollars! They ask him
to make again it every year.

Cranberry-Pear Streusel Pie

Debbi Blundi
Kunkletown, PA
I created this light and tasty pie for the hearty Italian pasta meals my husband's family enjoys. It's perfect for our church's Sunday potluck luncheons too.

1 c. sweetened dried cranberries, chopped
1-1/2 c. orange juice
9-inch deep-dish pie crust, unbaked
1/3 c. sugar
1/4 c. all-purpose flour
1 t. pumpkin pie spice
3 15-oz. cans sliced pears, drained

Combine cranberries and orange juice in a bowl. Refrigerate for several hours; drain. Bake pie crust at 350 degrees until lightly golden, about 15 minutes; cool. In a large bowl, mix sugar, flour and spice; add pears and cranberries. Pour into crust. Spread streusel topping evenly over pie. Bake at 350 degrees until golden, 30 to 40 minutes. Serves 6 to 8.

Streusel Topping:

1 c. all-purpose flour
1/2 c. brown sugar, packed
1 t. orange extract
1/2 c. chilled butter

Mix together all ingredients with a fork until crumbly.

Fresh Strawberry Pie

1-1/2 c. water
1 c. sugar
3 T. cornstarch
1/8 t. salt
3-oz. pkg. strawberry gelatin mix
1 T. lemon juice
1 t. red food coloring
4 c. fresh strawberries, hulled
    and sliced
9-inch pie crust, baked, or
    graham cracker crust
Optional: whipped cream

In a saucepan over medium heat,
combine water, sugar, cornstarch
and salt. Bring to a boil. Boil for
3 to 4 minutes, until mixture is
clear. Stir in dry gelatin mix, lemon
juice and food coloring. Remove
from heat and set aside to cool.
Arrange strawberries in baked crust.
Pour cooled gelatin mixture over
berries. Cover and refrigerate until
set. Top with whipped cream, if
desired. Serves 8.

51

Eva Jo Hoyle
Mexico, MO
My family loves strawberries
in the springtime. I love to
make this fresh strawberry
pie for them.

Peanut Butter Pie

Karen Hood Keeney
Bronston, KY

This pie is so good! My mother requests it often. I made it often in my sweet shop, Karen's Konfections. It is easy to prepare and so delicious.

1 c. powdered sugar
1/2 c. creamy peanut butter
9-inch deep-dish pie crust, baked
2/3 c. sugar
1/4 c. cornstarch
1/4 t. salt
3 egg yolks
2 c. milk
2 T. butter
1 t. vanilla extract

Mix powdered sugar and peanut butter with a fork until crumbly. Set aside 1/4 cup of mixture. Spread remaining mixture evenly in bottom and up sides of warm crust. In a saucepan over medium heat, cook sugar, cornstarch, salt, egg yolks and milk until thickened. Remove from heat; stir in butter and vanilla. Pour into crust. Spread meringue over filling, sealing to edges; top with reserved crumb mixture. Bake at 350 degrees for 8 to 10 minutes, until meringue is golden. Serves 8.

Meringue:

3 egg whites
1/4 t. cream of tartar
6 T. sugar

With an electric mixer on high speed, beat egg whites and cream of tartar until soft peaks form. Gradually beat in sugar; beat until glossy and stiff.

Frosty Butter Pecan Crunch Pie

2 c. graham cracker crumbs
1/2 c. butter, melted
2 3.4-oz. pkgs. instant vanilla
  pudding mix
2 c. milk
1 qt. butter pecan ice cream,
  slightly softened
8-oz. container frozen whipped
  topping, thawed
2 1.4-oz. chocolate-covered
  toffee candy bars, crushed

Combine graham cracker crumbs
and melted butter in a bowl; pat
into an ungreased 13"x9" baking
pan. Freeze until firm. In a large
bowl with an electric mixer on
medium speed, beat together dry
pudding mix and milk until well
blended, about one minute. Fold in
ice cream and whipped topping;
spoon over chilled crust. Sprinkle
with candy bar pieces; freeze. Remove
from freezer 20 minutes before
serving. Serves 12 to 15.

53

Lisa Johnson
Hallsville, TX

Chocolate and toffee come
together sweetly in this
scrumptious frozen pie.

Upside-Down Apple-Pecan Pie

1/2 c. butter, softened
1-1/2 c. pecan halves
1-1/2 c. brown sugar, packed
2 9-inch pie crusts, unbaked
1/2 c. sugar
2 T. lemon juice
1 t. vanilla extract
3 T. all-purpose flour
1 T. apple pie spice
1-1/8 t. cinnamon
1/2 t. nutmeg
3 c. Honey Crisp apples, peeled,
   cored and sliced
3 c. Swiss Gourmet apples,
   peeled, cored and sliced

Spread butter in the bottom and up the sides of a 9" deep-dish pie plate. Arrange pecans over butter, flat-side up, to cover pie plate. Sprinkle brown sugar over pecans. Place one crust on top; press into pie plate. In a large bowl, combine sugar, lemon juice, vanilla, flour and spices; mix well. Add apples; toss until coated. Spoon apple mixture evenly into crust. Add remaining crust. Fold over edges and crimp together; pierce several times with a fork. Bake at 450 degrees for 10 minutes. Reduce heat to 350 degrees; bake for another 45 minutes. Remove from oven; let stand until bubbling stops. While pie is still hot, invert a plate over pie and flip pie over onto plate. Pecans are now on top. Serve warm. Serves 8.

Francine Bryson
Pickens, SC

Both my grandmothers used to make this pie. Over the years, I tweaked it and even won the North Carolina State Apple Cook-Off Grand Champion with it!

Country Harvest Pie

2 9-inch pie crusts, unbaked
3 McIntosh apples, peeled, cored
  and thickly sliced
3 Bartlett pears, peeled, cored
  and sliced
3/4 c. fresh cranberries
3/4 c. sugar
3 T. all-purpose flour
1/4 t. cinnamon
1 T. milk
2 t. butter, sliced
Optional: whipped cream or
  vanilla ice cream

Place one pie crust in a 9" pie plate;
set aside. Combine fruits in a large
bowl; set aside. In a small bowl, mix
together flour and cinnamon;
combine with fruit mixture. Sprinkle
milk over fruit mixture; stir well.
Spoon into unbaked pie crust; dot
with butter. Add top crust; crimp
edges and cut several vents. Bake at
425 degrees for 15 minutes. Reduce
oven to 350 degrees. Continue
baking for 35 to 45 minutes, until
apples are tender. Garnish with
whipped cream or ice cream,
if desired. Serves 6 to 8.

Janis Parr
Campbellford, Ontario
This pie looks and tastes
wonderful. The cranberries
give it color and complement
the sweet mellowness of
the apples and pears.
Everyone loves it!

55

Nan's Chocolate Pie

1 c. sugar
3 T. cornstarch
1/3 c. baking cocoa
1/4 t. salt
1-1/2 c. milk
3 egg yolks, beaten
1/4 c. butter
1 t. vanilla extract
1/2 t. almond extract
9-inch pie crust, baked
Garnish: whipped cream,
  chocolate curls

In a saucepan, combine sugar, cornstarch, cocoa and salt; gradually stir in milk. Cook and stir over medium-high heat until bubbly; do not boil. Cook and stir an additional 2 minutes; remove from heat. Stir a small amount of hot mixture into egg yolks. Immediately add yolk mixture to saucepan and cook 2 minutes over low heat, stirring constantly. Remove from heat. Add butter and extracts; stir until smooth. Pour into baked pie crust. Chill; garnish with whipped cream and chocolate curls. Serves 8.

Becky Ladd
Delaware, OH

The most delicious chocolate pie ever! This recipe belonged to my grandmother. She was such a wonderful cook, and an excellent seamstress too.

Golden Tequila Lime Tart

Vickie

This fresh and summery tart is sure to be a winner at your next backyard cookout or Mexican feast!

12 graham crackers, crushed
1/4 c. pine nuts
3 T. sugar, divided
1/2 c. butter, melted
14-oz. can sweetened
   condensed milk
1/2 c. lime juice
1/4 c. gold tequila or
   lemon-lime soda
4 egg yolks
2 egg whites

Process crackers finely in a food processor. Measure out 1-1/2 cups; set aside. Finely process nuts and 2 tablespoons sugar; stir nut mixture and butter into crumbs. Press mixture evenly into bottom and up sides of an ungreased 9-1/2" round tart pan. In a large bowl, whisk together condensed milk, lime juice, tequila or soda and egg yolks until well blended. In a separate large bowl, beat egg whites and remaining sugar with an electric mixer on high speed until soft peaks form. Add 1/4 of egg white mixture to milk mixture; gently fold in remaining mixture and spoon into crust. Bake at 325 degrees for 25 to 30 minutes, until center is set and edges of filling are puffed and light golden. Cool completely; chill for 2 hours. Serves 12.

57

Raspberry Custard Pie

2 eggs, beaten
8-oz. container sour cream
1-1/2 to 2 c. fresh raspberries
1 c. sugar
1 T. all-purpose flour
1/2 t. salt
9-inch pie crust, unbaked

Whisk together eggs and sour cream in a large bowl; set aside. In a separate bowl, combine raspberries, sugar, flour and salt; toss lightly. Add berry mixture to sour cream mixture; mix well and pour into unbaked crust. Bake at 350 degrees for 45 minutes, until firm and golden. Cool completely. Serves 6 to 8.

Sarah Swanson
Noblesville, IN

Our five-year-old daughter collected raspberries every day for a week and wanted to bake a pie. So we made this pie...she & our other kids loved it!

Rustic Country Cherry Pie

6 T. butter, softened
1-1/2 c. all-purpose flour
2 to 3 T. cold water
1 egg, separated
2 T. cornmeal
1-1/2 lbs. fresh sour cherries,
  pitted
1/2 c. plus 1-1/2 T. sugar,
  divided

In a bowl, rub butter into flour with your fingertips until crumbly. Add water, one tablespoon at a time, until a dough begins to form. Knead dough for one minute; wrap in plastic wrap and chill for 30 minutes. Roll out dough on a floured surface into a 14-inch circle. Roll dough around rolling pin; transfer to a lightly greased baking sheet. Brush with beaten egg yolk; dust with cornmeal. Pile cherries in the center; sprinkle with 1/2 cup sugar. Fold in edges of dough 2 inches over cherries; brush dough with beaten egg white and sprinkle with remaining sugar. Bake at 350 degrees on top oven shelf until bubbly and crust is golden, about 35 to 40 minutes. Serves 6 to 8.

Michaela Topalov
Sidney, OH

Long before my best friend Beth and I had husbands and families, we were roommates. I still remember how we laughed when she taught me, a hopeless cook, how to make this delicious pie!

Sour Cream Lemon Pie

9-inch pie crust, baked
1 to 1-1/2 c. raspberry preserves
3-1/2 T. cornstarch
1 c. sugar
3/4 c. lemon juice
1 c. milk
3 egg yolks, beaten
1/4 c. butter, sliced
3/4 c. sour cream
1 c. whipping cream
1 T. vanilla extract
1/2 c. powdered sugar

In the bottom and sides of baked, cooled pie crust, spread preserves; set aside. In a microwave-safe dish, mix cornstarch and sugar. Add lemon juice, milk and egg yolks; whisk well. Microwave on high for one to 2-minute intervals, until mixture is very thick. Stir in butter, then sour cream. Pour mixture into pie crust; cool completely in refrigerator. With an electric mixer on high speed, beat cream until soft peaks form. Add vanilla and powdered sugar; beat until stiff peaks form. Spread over chilled pie. Serves 8.

Tara Johnson
Logan, UT

I won second place in a cooking competition with this pie. I added the raspberry preserves...now I have to make two to bring to Thanksgiving dinner!

Mini Pie Bites

15-oz. pkg. frozen pie crusts,
 thawed and unbaked
1 c. favorite-flavor fruit pie
 filling
1 T. milk
1/2 c. powdered sugar

Unroll pie crusts; cut each crust
into 12 equal squares. Spoon one to
2 teaspoons pie filling into the center
of each square. Bring the corners of
each square together above filling;
pinch together corners and seams
to seal. Place each mini pie into an
ungreased muffin cup. Bake at
450 degrees for 11 to 14 minutes,
until golden; cool. Meanwhile,
in a bowl, slowly whisk milk into
powdered sugar until a glaze
consistency is reached. Using a fork,
drizzle glaze over bites. Let stand for
about 20 minutes before serving.
Makes 2 dozen.

61

Krissy Mosqueda
Houston, TX

One of my favorite desserts!
I love that you can
customize it and make a
dozen different flavors if
you want to. It's quick,
easy, delicious and fun!

Gingersnap Pumpkin Pie

Sarah Phillip
Jamesburg, NJ

A delicious combination! I tried this recipe for Thanksgiving because I am not a big fan of ordinary pie crust...it was a huge hit with my family.

15-oz. can pumpkin
14-oz. can sweetened condensed milk
2 eggs, beaten
1/8 t. salt
2 T. plus 1/2 t. pumpkin pie spice, divided

In a bowl, blend pumpkin and condensed milk. Add eggs, salt and 2 tablespoons spice; mix well. Pour into Gingersnap Crust; sprinkle with remaining spice. Bake at 425 degrees for 15 minutes. Cover edges of crust with strips of aluminum foil, if browning too fast. Reduce oven to 350 degrees and bake for another 35 minutes, or until set. Cool before slicing. Serves 8.

Gingersnap Crust:

1-1/2 c. gingersnaps, crushed
Optional: 2 T. hazelnuts, crushed
3/4 c. butter, melted

Toss cookie crumbs and nuts, if using, with butter. Press into the bottom and up the sides of a 9" pie plate.

Fabulous Sweet Potato Pie

**Carma Sheffler
Seguin, TX**
I never liked sweet potatoes
'til I had this pie...it's
wonderful! It definitely
deserves a big dollop of
real whipped cream.

1/2 c. chopped pecans
9-inch pie crust, unbaked
1-1/2 c. cooked sweet potatoes
2/3 c. sweetened condensed milk
6 T. butter, softened
1 egg
1 t. vanilla extract
1 c. sugar
1-1/2 T. all-purpose flour
1 t. cinnamon
1/2 t. nutmeg
1/8 t. salt

Spread pecans in unbaked pie crust. Bake at 475 degrees for 5 minutes; cool. Reduce oven to 300 degrees. Beat sweet potatoes and butter with an electric mixer on medium speed until smooth. Beat in remaining ingredients. Pour into crust. Cover edges with aluminum foil. Bake at 300 degrees for 35 minutes. Sprinkle with topping; re-cover edges with foil. Bake for 30 minutes more, or until golden. Serve warm. Serves 8.

Topping:
2/3 c. chopped pecans
3 T. butter, melted
1/2 c. brown sugar, packed
1/3 c. all-purpose flour

Stir pecans into butter. Mix brown sugar and flour; add to pecans and toss lightly.

63

Apricot Pockets

Sandy Taranto
North Haledon, NJ

These little pockets are my favorite treat...they melt in your mouth!

1/2 c. butter, softened
3-oz. pkg. cream cheese, softened
1 c. all-purpose flour
15-oz. can apricot halves, drained
1 c. sugar
Garnish: powdered sugar or powdered sugar glaze

Blend together butter, cream cheese and flour; form into a ball. Wrap in plastic wrap; refrigerate overnight. Work dough until soft; roll out thinly on a floured surface. Cut dough into twelve 3-inch squares. For each pocket, roll an apricot half in sugar; place on a dough square and fold up corners to the center to form a pocket. Place pockets on a parchment paper-lined baking sheet. Bake at 350 degrees for 20 to 25 minutes, until lightly golden. Cool; dust with powdered sugar or drizzle with glaze. Makes one dozen.

Isabella's Ice Cream Pie

Payten Smith
Bellevue, OH

In memory of my Grandmother
Isabella, who won a cooking
contest with this recipe.

2 c. bite-size crispy rice cereal
squares, crushed
1 c. brown sugar, packed
1/2 c. sweetened flaked coconut
1/2 c. chopped almonds
1/2 c. butter, softened
1/2 gal. vanilla ice cream,
softened
1 pt. orange, raspberry or lime
sherbet, softened
Optional: candy sprinkles

In a large bowl, combine cereal,
brown sugar, coconut, almonds and
butter. Blend well; press into an
ungreased 13"x9" baking pan. Cover
and chill well. Spread ice cream in
crust; top with sherbet. Cover and
freeze until set. Cut into squares.
Garnish with sprinkles, if desired.
Serves 12 to 15.

65

Connie's Coconut Kentucky Pie

1 c. sugar
1/2 c. butter, melted
1/2 c. all-purpose flour
2 eggs, beaten
3/4 c. semi-sweet chocolate chips
1/2 c. sweetened flaked coconut
9-inch pie crust, unbaked
Optional: vanilla ice cream or
    whipped cream

Combine all ingredients except crust
and optional garnish in a bowl. Stir
together well and pour into unbaked
pie crust. Bake at 325 degrees for
45 minutes, or until set. Serve warm
or cooled, garnished as desired.
Makes 8 servings.

Pat Beach
Fisherville, KY
My minister's wife gave me
this recipe 30 years ago.
It's a lot like another pie
we serve around Derby time
in Kentucky, made with
coconut instead of pecans!

Mock Apple Pie

4 c. zucchini, peeled and
   chopped
2 T. lemon juice
1/8 t. salt
1-1/4 c. sugar
1-1/2 t. cream of tartar
3 T. all-purpose flour
1-1/2 t. cinnamon
1/8 t. nutmeg
2 9-inch pie crusts, unbaked

Cover zucchini with water in a large saucepan. Cook over medium heat until tender; drain well. In a bowl, combine remaining ingredients except pie crusts; mix well and stir in zucchini. Place one crust in a 9" pie plate; spoon in filling. Cover with top crust; crimp crust and cut vents with a knife. Bake at 400 degrees for 40 minutes, until bubbly and crust is golden. Makes 6 to 8 servings.

67

Melissa Barden
Otsego, MI

I won a blue ribbon for
this zucchini pie at the
county fair...I keep it
on my refrigerator to
remind my family that
I do know how to cook!

Rustic Pear Tart

Melody Taynor
Everett, WA
Simple to make, this recipe can make one large or many bite-size tarts.

1 c. plus 2 T. all-purpose flour, divided
1/4 c. plus 4 t. sugar, divided
1/4 t. baking powder
1/4 t. salt
1/4 c. plus 1 t. chilled butter, diced and divided
3 T. sour cream
1-1/2 lbs. pears, peeled, cored and sliced
1 T. lemon juice
1/2 t. vanilla extract
Garnish: powdered sugar

Mix one cup flour, one teaspoon sugar, baking powder and salt. Cut in 1/4 cup butter until mixture resembles coarse meal. Add sour cream; stir with a fork until very crumbly. Cover and chill for 30 minutes. Combine pears and lemon juice, 1/4 cup sugar and vanilla; toss to coat. On a lightly floured surface, roll out dough to a 14-inch circle; place on an ungreased baking sheet. Mix remaining flour and sugar; sprinkle evenly over dough. Arrange pear slices on top. Moisten dough edges with water; fold in edges 2 inches over pears. Dot with remaining butter. Bake at 400 degrees for 40 minutes, or until crust is golden. Cool 15 minutes; dust with powdered sugar.
Serves 6 to 8.

Berry-Rhubarb Pie

2 9-inch pie crusts, unbaked
1 T. all-purpose flour
2 T. instant tapioca, uncooked
1-1/4 c. sugar
1/2 t. cinnamon
2-1/2 c. rhubarb, chopped
1-1/2 c. fresh strawberries,
   hulled and chopped
1-1/2 c. fresh blackberries
1/2 t. lime zest
1 t. lime juice
1 t. vanilla extract
2 T. butter, diced
1 egg white
1 t. water

Arrange one pie crust in a 9-inch pie
plate; set aside. Combine flour,
tapioca, sugar and cinnamon. In a
separate bowl, combine rhubarb,
berries, zest, juice and vanilla. Add
flour mixture; stir gently to coat
fruit. Spoon fruit into crust; dot with
butter. Cover with remaining crust;
pinch to seal and cut vents. Whisk
together egg white and water; brush
over crust. Bake at 375 degrees for
50 to 60 minutes, until crust is
golden. Serves 8.

Nichole Leighton
Montgomery, AL
My husband loves rhubarb, so
when the season comes it's
an endless parade of rhubarb
dishes. I just made up this
new version. Now we have
a pie we love more than
any other!

Osgood Pie

3 eggs
1 c. sugar
6 T. butter, melted and
    cooled slightly
1 c. chopped pecans
1 c. raisins
1 T. vinegar
1 t. vanilla extract
1/8 t. ground cloves
1/8 t. cinnamon
1/8 t. nutmeg
9-inch pie crust, unbaked

Beat eggs in a large bowl. Add sugar
and butter; beat well. Stir in
remaining ingredients except crust.
Spoon into unbaked pie crust. Bake
at 350 degrees for one hour, or
until set. Cool completely. Makes
6 servings.

Sandra Monroe
Preston, MD

My mother served this pie for
many years and our family
still loves it. I took this
to work when we had a pie
contest and this recipe won!
It is so easy to make.

Sweet Cherry Triangles

Carrie O'Shea
Marina Del Rey, CA
Yummy...like biting into
a mini cherry pie!

1-1/4 c. all-purpose flour
1/4 t. salt
1 t. sugar, divided
1/2 c. butter, diced
2 to 3 T. cold water
15-oz. can dark sweet cherries,
   drained
1/4 c. cherry preserves
3/4 t. cinnamon, divided
2 eggs, beaten and divided

Mix together flour, salt and
1/2 teaspoon sugar. Cut in butter
with a pastry blender. Add water,
one tablespoon at a time, until a
dough forms. Wrap in plastic wrap;
refrigerate for one hour. On a
floured surface, roll out dough into
a 12-inch by 8-inch rectangle; cut
into six 4-inch squares. Stir together
cherries, preserves and 1/2 teaspoon
cinnamon. Spoon cherry mixture
equally onto each square. Brush
edges of squares with half of beaten
egg; fold into triangles. Seal edges
with a fork. Brush tops with
remaining egg; sprinkle with
remaining sugar and cinnamon.
Place on a lightly greased baking
sheet. Bake at 425 degrees for
15 minutes, or until golden. Makes
6 servings.

71

Grandma Katie's Glacé Pie

4 c. fresh blueberries, divided
1 c. water, divided
1 c. sugar
3 T. cornstarch
9-inch pie crust, baked

In a saucepan over low heat, combine one cup blueberries and 2/3 cup water. Simmer for about 5 minutes; stir. Add sugar, cornstarch and remaining water; boil for one minute, stirring constantly. Cool slightly. Put 2 cups blueberries into baked pie crust; pour cooked mixture over blueberries. Top with remaining blueberries. Cover and chill until serving time. Makes 8 servings.

Suzy Brugger Kanode
Weyers Cave, VA

I still remember picking blueberries with my grandma and mother. This is by far the most scrumptious pie I make!

Honey Pumpkin Pie

2 eggs
15-oz. can pumpkin
3/4 c. honey
1/2 t. salt
1 t. cinnamon
1/2 t. ginger
1/8 t. ground cloves
1 c. regular or fat-free evaporated milk
9-inch pie crust, unbaked
Garnish: whipped cream

In a bowl, beat eggs slightly. Add remaining ingredients except crust; stir well. Pour mixture into unbaked pie crust. Bake at 425 degrees for 15 minutes. Reduce heat to 350 degrees; bake an additional 45 minutes, or until filling is set. Cool; garnish with whipped cream. Makes 8 servings.

73

Sharon Velenosi
Costa Mesa, CA

Since my husband must avoid refined sugar, I've tried to make his favorite recipes using honey. This is a new version of one of his favorites.

Raspberry-Almond Kuchen

Connie Litfin
Carrollton, TX

I make this dessert all year 'round. It has been a family favorite for over 30 years. It is pretty enough for company!

1 egg, beaten
1/2 c. milk
1/2 c. sugar
2 T. oil
1 t. almond extract
1 c. all-purpose flour
2 t. baking powder
1 c. fresh raspberries
1/2 c. sliced almonds

In a large bowl, combine egg, milk, sugar, oil and extract. Add flour and baking powder; mix well. Spread batter in a greased 8"x8" baking pan. Sprinkle raspberries, crumb topping and almonds over batter. Bake at 375 degrees for 25 to 30 minutes. Cut into squares; serve warm. Serves 9.

Crumb Topping:
3/4 c. all-purpose flour
1/2 c. sugar
3 T. chilled butter

Mix flour and sugar; cut in butter with a fork until crumbly.

Royal Strawberry Shortcake

1/4 c. butter, softened
3/4 c. sugar
1 egg, beaten
2 c. all-purpose flour
4 t. baking powder
1/8 t. salt
1 c. milk
2 t. vanilla extract
3 to 4 c. fresh strawberries,
   hulled and sliced
Optional: softened cream cheese
Garnish: whipped cream

In a large bowl, blend together butter and sugar. Add egg; mix well. In a separate bowl, combine flour, baking powder and salt. Add flour mixture to butter mixture alternately with milk. Stir in vanilla. Spread batter in a greased 13"x9" baking pan. Bake at 350 degrees for 25 to 30 minutes. Cool; cut shortcake into squares and split. Place bottom halves of shortcake squares on dessert plates. Spread with cream cheese, if desired; top with strawberries and whipped cream. Add shortcake tops and more berries and cream. Serves 10 to 12.

Becky Smith
North Canton, OH
This recipe was passed down from my Grandma Emma. Whenever my sisters & I came back from berry-picking, Mom would bake up this wonderful dessert for supper.

75

Country Rhubarb Crunch

1 c. plus 2 T. all-purpose flour,
   divided
2 c. sugar, divided
1 T. butter, diced
4 c. rhubarb, sliced
1 t. baking powder
1/4 t. salt
1 egg, beaten
Garnish: vanilla ice cream

In a large bowl, mix together
2 tablespoons flour, one cup sugar,
butter and rhubarb. Spoon into an
ungreased 8"x8" baking pan. In a
separate bowl, mix together
remaining flour, remaining sugar,
baking powder and salt. Stir in egg.
Mixture will be crumbly. Sprinkle
over rhubarb mixture; shake pan so
crumbs settle into rhubarb. Bake at
350 degrees for 40 minutes, or until
crust is lightly golden. Serve warm or
cold, topped with scoops of vanilla
ice cream. Makes 8 servings.

Terri Clark
Huber Heights, OH

My grandma made this for
all of us back in the
50s and 60s. Grandpa loved
rhubarb and after Grandma
found this recipe, we loved
it too. We still enjoy it.

Blueberry Buckle

1-1/4 c. sugar, divided
1/2 c. butter, softened
  and divided
1 egg, beaten
1/2 c. milk
2-1/3 c. all-purpose flour,
  divided
2 t. baking powder
1/2 t. salt
2 c. fresh blueberries
1/2 t. cinnamon

Mix 3/4 cup sugar, 1/4 cup butter and egg; stir in milk. Sift together 2 cups flour, baking powder and salt; add to batter. Blend in blueberries. Spread batter in a greased 9"x9" baking pan. In a separate bowl, mix cinnamon and remaining sugar, flour and butter until crumbly. Sprinkle cinnamon mixture over blueberry mixture. Bake at 375 degrees for 35 to 40 minutes, until bubbly and golden. Serves 9.

77

Karen Bernards
San Fernando, CA

A great treat at breakfast
or any time of day...
my family loves it!

Cranberry-Walnut Cobbler

2-1/2 c. fresh or frozen
    cranberries
3/4 c. chopped walnuts
1/2 c. plus 3/4 c. sugar, divided
2 eggs, beaten
3/4 c. butter, melted and slightly
    cooled
1/4 t. almond extract
1 c. all-purpose flour
1/8 t. salt

In an ungreased 9" pie plate,
combine cranberries, walnuts and
1/2 cup sugar. Toss until coated; set
aside. In a bowl, whisk together eggs,
melted butter, remaining sugar and
extract until blended. Fold in flour
and salt until combined. Pour batter
over cranberry mixture. Bake at
350 degrees for 40 minutes, or until
bubbly and crust is golden. Transfer
to a wire rack to cool. Serves 8.

Kathy Grashoff
Fort Wayne, IN

Crisp fall days make me
eager to begin baking again.
Nothing says fall like
cranberries and walnuts!

Aunt Marge's Peachy Pineapple Dessert

20-oz. can crushed pineapple
29-oz. can sliced peaches
18-1/2 oz. pkg. white or yellow
  cake mix
1/2 to 1 c. chopped walnuts
  or pecans
3/4 to 1 c. butter, melted

In an ungreased 13"x9" glass baking
pan, evenly spread pineapple with
juices; add peaches with juices.
Sprinkle with dry cake mix, then
with nuts. Drizzle with melted butter;
do not stir. Bake at 350 degrees for
35 to 40 minutes, until bubbly and
top is lightly golden. Serve warm.
Serves 10 to 12.

Marilyn Just
De Soto, KS

This recipe is at least
50 years old. It was handed
down to my mom from a very
close family friend we
called Aunt Marge. It was my
favorite dessert growing up.

French Pear Pudding

8-oz. container sour cream
1 egg, lightly beaten
1 t. vanilla extract
2 T. sugar
1/3 c. plus 1 T. all-purpose flour,
   divided
15-oz. can pear halves, drained
   and quartered
1/4 c. brown sugar, packed
1/2 t. nutmeg
2 T. butter

In a bowl, combine sour cream, egg and vanilla. In a cup, mix sugar and one tablespoon flour; add to sour cream mixture and stir well. Arrange pears in an ungreased shallow one-quart casserole dish; top with sour cream mixture. Bake at 350 degrees for 15 minutes. In a separate bowl, combine brown sugar, remaining flour and nutmeg. Cut in butter with a pastry blender until mixture resembles cornmeal. Sprinkle over sour cream mixture; bake an additional 15 minutes. Makes 6 servings.

Kathleen Walker
Mountain Center, CA

A favorite of my family
and a must on the
holiday table!

Quebec Maple Bread Pudding

3 c. egg bread or white bread,
   cubed
Optional: 1/2 c. chopped pecans
   or walnuts
3 c. milk
1 c. brown sugar, packed
4 eggs, beaten
1 t. vanilla extract
2 T. butter, sliced
Garnish: pure maple syrup

Place bread cubes in a greased
9"x9" baking pan. Sprinkle with
nuts, if using; set aside. Combine
milk and brown sugar in a saucepan
over medium-low heat; stir until
hot and sugar is dissolved. Remove
from heat. Whisk in eggs; stir in
vanilla. Pour milk mixture over
bread, soaking thoroughly. Dot with
butter. Bake at 350 degrees for
one hour, or until set. Serve warm,
drizzled generously with maple syrup.
Serves 4.

81

Mitzy LaFrenais-Hafner
Dollard Des Ormeaux,
Quebec

This bread pudding is cozy,
quick & easy comfort food...
wonderful when you are
snowed in!

Prize Peanut Butter-Chocolate Dessert

20 chocolate sandwich cookies, divided
2 T. butter, melted
8-oz. pkg. cream cheese, softened
1/2 c. creamy peanut butter
1-1/2 c. powdered sugar, divided
16-oz. container frozen whipped topping, thawed and divided
15 mini peanut butter cups, chopped
1 c. cold milk
3.9-oz. pkg. instant chocolate fudge pudding mix

Crush 16 cookies; toss with butter. Press into the bottom of an ungreased 9"x9" baking pan. In a bowl, beat cream cheese, peanut butter and one cup powdered sugar until smooth. Fold in half of the whipped topping; spread over crust. Sprinkle with peanut butter cups. In a separate bowl, beat milk, dry pudding mix and remaining powdered sugar on low speed for 2 minutes. Fold in remaining topping; spread over peanut butter cups. Crush remaining cookies; sprinkle over top. Cover and chill at least 3 hours. Serves 12 to 15.

Deborah Price
La Rue, OH

I won the Grand Prize in a national cooking magazine with this recipe! I don't dare show up at a family event without it.

Julie's Strawberry Yum-Yum

2 3.3-oz. pkgs. instant
   sugar-free white chocolate
   pudding mix
4 c. 1% milk
1 baked angel food cake,
   torn into bite-size pieces
   and divided
2 to 4 c. fresh strawberries,
   hulled, sliced and divided
2 8-oz. containers fat-free
   frozen whipped topping,
   thawed
10-oz. pkg. coconut macaroon
   cookies, crushed and divided

Beat dry pudding mix and milk with
an electric mixer on low speed for
2 minutes. Chill for a few minutes,
until thickened. In a large trifle bowl,
layer half each of cake pieces, pudding
and strawberries, one container
whipped topping and half of crushed
cookies. Repeat layers, ending with
cookies. Cover and chill until serving
time. Makes 8 to 10 servings.

83

Julie Hutson
Callahan, FL

A wonderful, lighter
strawberry trifle that's a
snap to put together...this
recipe is a winner!

Spiced Cranberry-Apple Crisp

4 Golden Delicious apples,
   peeled, cored and sliced
1 c. fresh cranberries
3/4 c. light brown sugar, packed
1/2 c. all-purpose flour
1/2 c. rolled oats, uncooked
3/4 t. cinnamon
3/4 t. nutmeg
1/3 c. butter, softened
Garnish: ice cream or whipped
   cream

Combine apples and cranberries in
a buttered 8"x8" baking pan; set
aside. In a bowl, combine remaining
ingredients except garnish. Mix well
and sprinkle over fruit. Bake at
375 degrees for 30 minutes, or until
top is golden. Serve warm; garnish
with ice cream or whipped cream.
Makes 6 servings.

Arlene Smulski
Lyons, IL
I have made this fall dessert
many times and it never
fails. No matter what kind
of apples you use, it will
come out perfectly!

Strawberry-Nectarine Cobbler

Alisha Jhai
West Dundee, IL

For the past ten years I've made this cobbler every summer, when the fresh fruit is best. It is sweet, refreshing and an instant friend-maker. Top with ice cream, if you like.

6 to 8 nectarines, pitted and very
   thinly sliced
1/4 c. light brown sugar, packed
1 t. cinnamon
1/4 t. nutmeg
1 t. salt
2 c. fresh strawberries, hulled
   and halved or whole
2 T. butter, sliced
1/2 c. sugar, divided
1 egg, beaten
1 T. baking powder
1 c. all-purpose flour
1 T. vanilla extract
1/2 c. milk

85

Combine nectarines, brown sugar, spices and salt; let stand for 15 minutes. In a saucepan, combine strawberries, butter and 1/4 cup sugar. Cook and stir for 5 minutes, until syrupy. Remove from heat; cool. In a separate bowl, whisk remaining sugar, egg, baking powder, flour, vanilla and milk. Spread nectarine mixture evenly in an ungreased 13"x9" glass baking pan. Spoon strawberry mixture evenly over nectarines. Dollop with spoonfuls of batter. Bake at 350 degrees for 30 to 35 minutes. Cool at least 15 minutes. Serves 12.

Honey-Custard Bread Pudding

6 eggs
1/2 t. salt
4 c. milk
2/3 c. plus 2 T. honey, divided
2 T. butter, melted
Optional: 1/2 c. raisins
16-oz. loaf Vienna or French
    bread, torn into one-inch
    pieces

Beat together eggs and salt; set aside.
Bring milk just to a boil in a saucepan
over low heat; let cool slightly. Stir
2/3 cup honey and butter into milk.
Slowly stir eggs into milk mixture;
add raisins, if using. Place bread
pieces in a greased 2-1/2 quart
casserole dish. Pour egg mixture over
bread. Set casserole dish in a larger
pan; add hot water to the pan to
come halfway up the side of the
casserole dish. Bake at 325 degrees
for one hour, or until set. About
15 minutes before serving, drizzle
remaining honey over top. Makes 8
to 10 servings.

Rogene Rogers
Bemidji, MN
Everyone is sure to enjoy
this rich, old-fashioned
bread pudding.

Banana Split Trifle

3.4-oz. pkg. instant vanilla
  pudding mix
4 c. milk, divided
3.4-oz. pkg. instant chocolate
  pudding mix
60 vanilla wafers, divided
3 ripe bananas, sliced
6 T. chocolate syrup, divided
15-oz. can crushed pineapple,
  drained
8-oz. container frozen whipped
  topping, thawed
10 maraschino cherries, drained
1/4 c. chopped pecans

Whisk vanilla pudding mix with
2 cups milk for 2 minutes; let stand
until thickened. In a separate bowl,
whisk chocolate pudding mix with
remaining milk. In the bottom of a
large trifle bowl, arrange 30 vanilla
wafers. Spoon vanilla pudding over
wafers. Arrange sliced bananas over
pudding; drizzle with 3 tablespoons
syrup. Arrange remaining wafers on
top. Add pineapple; spoon chocolate
pudding over pineapple. Add
topping; spread to edges of bowl.
Cover; refrigerate overnight. Garnish
with cherries and pecans; drizzle with
remaining syrup. Serves 8 to 10.

Cynthia Aaron
Farmerville, LA

This scrumptious recipe is
mine. Family & friends are
always asking me to make
it for get-togethers!

German Apple Streusel Kuchen

1 loaf frozen bread dough,
   thawed
4 Granny Smith apples, cored,
   peeled and thinly sliced
3/4 c. plus 1/3 c. sugar, divided
1 t. cinnamon
1 T. vanilla extract
1/4 c. sliced almonds
1/4 c. butter, melted
1-1/4 c. all-purpose flour

Let dough rise according to package directions. Spread out dough on a greased 15"x10" jelly-roll pan. Let rise again for 20 to 25 minutes. Mix apples, 3/4 cup sugar, cinnamon and vanilla; spread apple mixture evenly over dough. Sprinkle with almonds; set aside. In a small bowl, combine butter, flour and remaining sugar; mix with fingertips or a fork until crumbly. Spread evenly over apple layer. Bake at 375 degrees for 25 minutes. Cut into squares to serve. Makes 24 servings.

Karin Anderson
Hillsboro, OH

I was born and raised in Germany. Baking this cake brings back so many beautiful memories of my parents and brothers.

Social Apple Betty

6 to 7 apples, peeled, cored,
   and sliced
cinnamon to taste
Optional: sugar to taste
1/2 c. butter, softened
1 c. brown sugar, packed
3/4 c. all-purpose flour

Arrange sliced apples in an ungreased
1-1/2 quart casserole dish, filling
2/3 full. Sprinkle with cinnamon to
taste. If apples are tart, add some
sugar, as desired. In a bowl, blend
butter and brown sugar. Add flour;
mix with a fork until crumbly.
Sprinkle butter mixture over apples;
pat firmly into a crust. Bake at
325 degrees for 40 minutes, or until
golden and apples are tender. Serve
warm. Serves 6.

89

Barb Rudyk
Vermilion, Alberta

Everyone loves this
old-fashioned recipe. Serve
it warm, with a dollop of
whipping cream or ice
cream...delicious!

Dessert Dumplings with Caramel Sauce

1-1/2 c. boiling water
1-1/2 c. brown sugar, packed
6 T. butter, divided
1-1/2 t. vanilla extract, divided
1/2 t. salt, divided
1-1/2 c. all-purpose flour
1-1/2 t. baking powder
1/3 c. sugar
2/3 c. milk

For caramel sauce, combine boiling water, brown sugar, 2 tablespoons butter, one teaspoon vanilla and 1/4 teaspoon salt in a large saucepan. Bring to a boil over medium-high heat, stirring until brown sugar dissolves. Meanwhile, in a bowl, combine flour, baking powder, sugar and remaining salt. Cut in remaining butter until mixture resembles coarse crumbs. Stir in milk and remaining vanilla to make a soft dough. Drop dough by heaping tablespoonfuls into boiling sauce. Reduce heat to medium-low; cover. Simmer for 15 minutes, or until dumplings are cooked through. Serve warm. Serves 6.

Pamela Berube
Columbus, OH

This is the ultimate comfort food dessert. My grandmother learned this recipe from her Italian mother, and it has remained a family favorite for generations.

Rhode Island Peach Slump

6 c. peaches, peeled, pitted
    and sliced
1 c. sugar
1-1/2 t. cinnamon
1/2 c. water
10 to 12 baking powder biscuits,
    baked
Garnish: whipping cream

Combine peaches, sugar, cinnamon
and water in a heavy skillet. Bring
to a boil over medium-high heat.
Reduce heat to medium; arrange
biscuits on top. Cover and simmer,
for 30 minutes. To serve, spoon
peach mixture into dessert bowls;
top each bowl with a biscuit. Drizzle
with cream just before serving.
Makes 10 to 12 servings.

91

Betty Riser
Mount Pleasant, RI

This old-fashioned dessert
with the funny name is
oh-so easy to make...so
delicious to eat!

Shiny-Top Blueberry Cobbler

5 to 6 c. fresh blueberries
1-1/2 T. lemon juice
2 c. all-purpose flour
2 c. sugar, divided
2 t. baking powder
1 t. salt, divided
1 c. milk
1/3 c. butter, diced
2 T. cornstarch
1-1/2 c. boiling water
Garnish: vanilla ice cream

Spread berries in a greased shallow 2-1/2 quart casserole dish. Sprinkle with lemon juice; set aside. In a bowl, combine flour, one cup sugar, baking powder, 1/2 teaspoon salt, milk and butter. Stir until well blended. Spoon batter over berries, spreading to edge of dish; set aside. In a small bowl, mix remaining sugar and salt with cornstarch. Sprinkle over batter. Pour boiling water over all; do not stir. Bake at 350 degrees for one hour, or until bubbly, golden and glazed. Serve warm or cooled, topped with ice cream. Serves 10 to 12.

Bonnie Russell
Dixon, CA

A friend shared this recipe many years ago. I won first prize at our May Fair cobbler baking contest with this dessert.

Wild Blackberry Cobbler

1/2 c. butter, sliced
3 c. fresh blackberries
1/4 c. plus 2 T. water, divided
1-1/4 c. sugar, divided
1/2 t. cinnamon
2 T. cornstarch
1 c. all-purpose flour
1-i/2 t. baking powder
1/4 t. salt
1 c. milk

Add butter to a 9"x9" baking pan. Place in oven at 400 degrees until melted. Meanwhile, in a small saucepan, combine blackberries, 1/4 cup water, 1/4 cup sugar and cinnamon. Simmer over medium heat, stirring gently. Stir together cornstarch and remaining water until pourable; stir into berry mixture and cook until thickened. Remove from heat. In a bowl, mix flour, remaining sugar, baking powder, salt and milk; stir until smooth. Add flour mixture to butter in baking pan; carefully add berry mixture. Bake at 400 degrees for 25 to 30 minutes, until bubbly and crust is golden. Serves 4 to 6.

Edith Beck
Elk Grove, CA

A very old recipe that a friend shared with me in high school. Every year, we pick wild blackberries together so I can make this cobbler.

Nathaniel's Chocolate Bowl

15-1/4 oz. pkg. devil's food
  cake mix
1 c. water
1/2 c. oil
3 eggs, beaten
2 3.4-oz. pkgs. instant chocolate
  pudding mix
4 c. milk
16-oz. container frozen whipped
  topping, thawed
1 c. mini semi-sweet chocolate
  chips

Prepare cake mix with water, oil and
eggs according to package directions;
bake in a 13"x9" baking pan. Cool
completely; cut into one-inch cubes.
Meanwhile, prepare pudding mixes
with milk according to package
directions. In a large glass trifle bowl,
layer half each of cake cubes, pudding
and whipped topping. Repeat layers,
ending with topping. Sprinkle with
chocolate chips. Cover and chill until
serving time. Serves 10 to 12.

Amy Hunt
Traphill, NC

This is my son's favorite
dessert. He requests it
for his birthday instead of
cake. Any day is a special
occasion to fix what your
family loves!

Peach-Blueberry Crisp

8 peaches, peeled, pitted
   and sliced
1 c. fresh blueberries
1 T. lemon juice
1/4 c. all-purpose flour
1/3 c. brown sugar, packed
2 T. sugar
1/2 t. vanilla extract

Combine all ingredients in a large
bowl; toss lightly. Spoon mixture into
an ungreased 9" deep-dish pie plate.
Add topping, breaking it up as you
put it on. Bake at 350 degrees for
20 to 25 minutes, until topping is
golden. Serves 8.

Topping:
1-1/4 c. all-purpose flour
1/2 c. rolled oats, uncooked
1/2 c. brown sugar, packed
1/2 c. sugar
1/2 c. plus 2 T. butter, melted

Mix all ingredients until crumbly.

95

Patricia Allen
Buckner, IL

I had a huge box of peaches
to use up, so I tossed this
together for my dad. Now I
use this scrumptious recipe
for any fruit I have on hand.

Granny's Chocolate Cobbler

3/4 c. butter, melted
3 c. sugar, divided
1-1/2 c. self-rising flour
1/2 c. milk
1/2 c. plus 2 T. baking cocoa, divided
2 t. vanilla extract
2-1/2 c. boiling water
Optional: fresh strawberries, coarse sugar

Spread melted butter in a 13"x9" baking pan; set aside. In a large bowl, combine 1-1/2 cups sugar, flour, milk, 2 tablespoons cocoa and vanilla. Pour over butter in pan. In a small bowl, mix remaining sugar and cocoa; sprinkle evenly over batter. Pour boiling water over batter; do not stir. Bake at 350 degrees for 30 minutes. Serve warm, garnished as desired. Makes 6 to 8 servings.

Lorrie Smith
Munford, TN

This recipe has been passed around my family for years. It's just too yummy for words...yet oh-so quick & easy to make!

Pineapple-Cherry Crisp

20-oz. can crushed pineapple,
  well drained
2 21-oz. cans cherry pie filling
18-1/2 oz. pkg. white cake mix
1/2 c. butter, thinly sliced
3/4 c. chopped pecans
Garnish: whipped cream or
  ice cream

Spread pineapple evenly in an
ungreased 13"x9" baking pan.
Pour pie filling over pineapple.
Sprinkle dry cake mix on top; dot
with butter and top with pecans.
Bake at 350 degrees for 45 minutes,
until bubbly and topping is golden.
Serve warm or cooled, garnished as
desired. Makes 12 to 15 servings.

97

Becky Holsinger
Belpre, OH
I found this recipe while
visiting Amish country. My
husband loved it, and he
doesn't care for desserts as
much as I do. Plus, it's
quick & easy to make. Can't
beat that!

Mom-Mom's Famous Apple Crisp

10 apples, peeled, cored
   and quartered
1 c. water

Arrange apple slices in an ungreased
8"x8" baking pan, filling pan tightly.
Pour water over apples; set aside.
Spoon topping over apples. Bake at
325 degrees for 1-1/2 to 2 hours,
until apples are very tender and
topping is golden. Makes 6 to 8
servings.

Topping:
3/4 c. brown sugar, packed
1 t. cinnamon
1/2 c. butter, softened

Combine ingredients; mix with a
pastry blender until crumbly.
Topping may be doubled for added
sweetness.

Marion Satterthwaite
Blairstown, NJ

My mother's recipe, passed
down to her daughters and
grandchildren. We all love
this recipe and always
asked her to make it. To
smell it baking brings back
many memories.

Sour Cream Kuchen

1 c. butter, softened
1 c. sugar
2 eggs, beaten
1 t. vanilla extract
2 c. all-purpose flour
1 t. baking powder
1 t. baking soda
1/2 t. salt
8-oz. container sour cream

In a large bowl, beat butter and sugar with an electric mixer on medium speed until smooth. Add remaining ingredients; mix well. Spread half of batter in an ungreased 13"x9" baking pan. Cover with half of topping. Repeat with remaining batter and topping. Bake at 350 degrees for 35 to 40 minutes, until a toothpick tests clean. Cool about 15 minutes. Serves 10 to 12.

Topping:
1/2 c. brown sugar, packed
1/3 c. sugar
2 t. cinnamon

Mix all ingredients well.

Catherine Blatnik
Okemos, MI
I found this recipe among my mother-in-law's recipes. She was a fabulous baker. My husband remembers eating this when he was young... and he's over 60! It's a favorite at our house.

99

Cinnamon Bread Pudding

6 eggs
2 c. milk
2 c. half-and-half, divided
1 c. sugar
2 t. vanilla extract
6 c. cinnamon bread, cubed
1/2 c. brown sugar, packed
1/4 c. butter
1/2 c. light corn syrup

Beat eggs in a large bowl; whisk in milk, 1-3/4 cups half-and-half, sugar and vanilla. Stir in bread cubes until lightly moistened. Spread mixture evenly in a greased 2-quart casserole dish. Bake at 325 degrees for 55 to 60 minutes, until center starts to firm. In a saucepan over medium-low heat, heat brown sugar and butter until butter melts. Stir in corn syrup and remaining half-and-half. Cook, stirring constantly, for one to 2 minutes, until smooth and brown sugar dissolves. Spoon sauce over warm pudding. Serves 8.

Sharon Gould
Howard City, MI

Cinnamon bread makes this dessert extra special, and the warm butter sauce drizzled over the top is oh-so good.

Virginia Apple Pudding

2-1/4 c. apples, peeled, cored
  and sliced
1/2 c. butter, sliced
1 c. sugar
1 c. all-purpose flour
2 t. baking powder
1/4 t. salt
1/4 t. cinnamon
1 c. milk
Garnish: whipped cream,
  ice cream or lemon sauce

In a saucepan, cover apples with water. Cook over medium-high heat just until tender, about 5 minutes; drain well. Place butter in a 2-quart casserole dish; melt in oven at 375 degrees. In a bowl, stir together remaining ingredients except garnish; pour over butter in dish. Do not stir. Spoon apples into center of batter; do not stir. Bake at 375 degrees for about 40 minutes, until batter covers fruit and crust forms. Serve warm or cold; garnish as desired. Serves 4 to 6.

101

**Jeannie Wolf
Findlay, OH**

My mom would make this in the fall when apples were plentiful. It was especially good on a chilly evening... I remember eating leftovers for breakfast too!

Creamy Coconut Bread Pudding

8-oz. pkg. cream cheese,
   room temperature
1 c. sugar
4 eggs, beaten
2 c. milk
15-oz. can cream of coconut
5 T. butter, melted and divided
1/2 loaf French bread, cubed
1/2 c. sweetened flaked coconut
1/2 c. chopped pecans
Garnish: whipped cream

In a large bowl, beat cream cheese until creamy. Add sugar and eggs; beat again. Stir in milk, cream of coconut and 2 tablespoons melted butter. Stir in bread cubes; let stand a few minutes, until moistened. Spoon mixture into a buttered 13"x9" baking pan. Bake at 350 degrees for 35 minutes; do not overbake. Combine coconut, pecans and remaining butter; sprinkle over top. Bake another 5 to 8 minutes, until golden. For best flavor, chill before serving. Garnish with whipped cream. Serves 12 to 15.

Patty Parker
Cabool, MO

If you like bread pudding or coconut cream pie, you will love this! I got this recipe from a friend and changed it 'til it was even yummier. I'm a retired home ec teacher so I love to try new recipes.

First-Prize Peach Cobbler

18-1/2 oz. pkg. yellow cake mix
29-oz. can sliced peaches
15-oz. can sliced peaches
1/2 c. half-and-half
1/2 c. sugar
1/2 c. butter, sliced
Garnish: whipped cream or
   vanilla ice cream

Add dry cake mix to a 13"x9" baking pan sprayed with non-stick vegetable spray. Make a well in the center of cake mix. Add undrained peaches and half-and-half; stir to blend and moisten. Sprinkle with sugar; dot with butter. Cover and refrigerate 8 hours to overnight to allow flavors to blend. Bake at 350 degrees for one hour, or until bubbly and golden. Serve warm or cold, garnished as desired. Makes 6 to 8 servings.

103

Debbie Desormeaux
Lafayette, LA

Our family loves this! It tastes great served warm or cold.

Pumpkin Custard Crunch

29-oz. can pumpkin
3 eggs, beaten
2 t. pumpkin pie spice
1 t. cinnamon
14-oz. can sweetened condensed
  milk
1 c. milk
2 t. vanilla extract

Mix pumpkin, eggs and spices well; stir in milks and vanilla. Pour into a greased 13"x9" baking pan; spoon crunch topping over pumpkin mixture. Bake at 350 degrees for 45 to 60 minutes, until a knife tip comes out clean. Watch carefully so that topping doesn't burn. Serve warm. Makes 9 to 12 servings.

Crunch Topping:

3 c. quick-cooking oats,
  uncooked
1 c. brown sugar, packed
1 c. all-purpose flour
1 t. cinnamon
1 c. walnuts or pecans, crushed
1 c. butter, melted

Stir together oats, brown sugar, flour, cinnamon and nuts. Add melted butter; toss to mix.

Donna Borton
Columbus, OH

I have made this festive dessert for years. Enjoy it plain or topped with ice cream like my husband does!

Cherry Crumb Dessert

1/2 c. butter, chilled
18-1/2 oz. pkg. yellow cake mix
21-oz. can cherry pie filling
1/2 c. chopped walnuts
Garnish: vanilla ice cream

In a large bowl, cut butter into dry cake mix until mixture resembles coarse crumbs. Set aside one cup of mixture for topping. Pat remaining mixture into the bottom of a greased 13"x9" baking pan and 1/2 inch up the sides to form a crust. Spread pie filling over crust. Combine nuts with remaining crumbs; sprinkle over top. Bake at 350 degrees for 30 to 35 minutes. Serve warm, topped with ice cream. Makes 12 servings.

105

Charlotte Smith
Alexandria, PA
Need a quick & easy dessert?
Try this...you probably have
most of the ingredients in
your pantry already!

Buttermilk Pear Cobbler

3 lbs. Anjou or Bosc pears,
  peeled, cored and sliced
1/3 c. brown sugar, packed
1 T. all-purpose flour
1 T. lemon juice
1 t. cinnamon
1/4 t. nutmeg
1/4 t. mace

Combine all ingredients in a large bowl. Toss gently and spoon into a lightly greased 8"x8" baking pan. Drop biscuit topping by heaping tablespoonfuls onto pear mixture. Bake at 350 degrees for 45 minutes, or until bubbly and lightly golden. Serves 8.

Biscuit Topping:

1 c. all-purpose flour
1 T. baking powder
2 T. sugar
3 T. buttermilk
1/2 c. cold butter
3/4 c. milk

Mix together flour, baking powder, sugar and buttermilk. Cut in butter with a fork until mixture is crumbly; add milk and mix well.

Trysha Mapley-Barron
Palmer, AK

This recipe was inspired by my Grandmother Doris. She likely made a similar dessert on her farm in upstate New York. It's absolute comfort food, perfect for fall or winter.

Cherries Jubilee Crisp

15-oz. can dark sweet cherries
2 T. orange liqueur or
   orange juice
2-1/2 t. cornstarch
1/4 c. quick-cooking oats,
   uncooked
6 T. all-purpose flour
1/4 c. brown sugar, packed
1/4 t. nutmeg
1/4 c. cold butter, diced
Optional: whipped cream,
   nutmeg

Combine undrained cherries, liqueur or juice and cornstarch in a saucepan. Cook and stir over medium heat about 2 minutes, until cornstarch dissolves and mixture thickens. Pour into a lightly greased one-quart casserole dish; let cool for 10 minutes. In a small bowl, stir together oats, flour, brown sugar and nutmeg. Add butter; mix with a fork until crumbly. Sprinkle oat mixture over cherry mixture. Bake at 375 degrees for about 20 minutes, until topping is golden. Serve warm, topped with whipped cream and a sprinkle of nutmeg, if desired. Serves 4.

107

Jill Valentine
Jackson, TN
I like to treat my family to a warm homemade dessert on weekends. This recipe makes just a few portions so it's sized right for small families.

INDEX

Cakes

Banana-Nut Cake, 19
Bee Sting Cake, 17
Blue-Ribbon Chocolate Cake, 16
Blue-Ribbon Pound Cake, 35
Blue-Ribbon Pumpkin Roll, 28
Blueberry Pound Cake, 10
Butterscotch Picnic Cake, 12
Cherry Loaf Cake, 22
County Fair Grand Champion Cake, 24
Cream Cheese Pound Cake, 33
Dad's Apple Cake, 29
Debby's Orange Sherbet Cake, 13
Fresh Apple Cake, 18
Fruit Cocktail Cake, 32
Grandma's Cherry Pudding Cake, 26
Holiday Orange Cake, 34
Judy's Prize-Winning Toasted Pecan Cake, 9
Kay's Carrot Cake, 20
Mocha Pudding Cake, 38
Nutmeg Feather Cake, 36
Oma's Lemon Cheesecake, 14
Peach Cobbler Muffins, 21
Pecan Pie Muffins, 27
Pineapple Sheet Cake, 25
Prize-Winning Almond Bundt Cake, 8
Red Velvet Cake, 23
Royal Strawberry Shortcake, 75
Strawberry Layer Cake, 15
Strawberry Shortcake Cake, 31
Summer Lemon Cake, 30
Tres Leches Cake, 11
Tried & True Bundt Cake, 37

Cobblers and Crisps

Aunt Marge's Peachy Pineapple Dessert, 79
Blueberry Buckle, 77
Buttermilk Pear Cobbler, 106
Cherries Jubilee Crisp, 107
Cherry Crumb Dessert, 105
Country Rhubarb Crunch, 76
Cranberry-Walnut Cobbler, 78
First-Prize Peach Cobbler, 103
Granny's Chocolate Cobbler, 96
Mom-Mom's Famous Apple Crisp, 98
Peach-Blueberry Crisp, 95
Pineapple-Cherry Crisp, 97
Pumpkin Custard Crunch, 104
Shiny-Top Blueberry Cobbler, 92
Social Apple Betty, 89
Spiced Cranberry-Apple Crisp, 84
Strawberry-Nectarine Cobbler, 85
Wild Blackberry Cobbler, 93

Coffee Cakes

Cherry Streusel Coffee Cake, 7
German Apple Streusel Kuchen, 88
Gram's Rhubarb Coffee Cake, 39
Raspberry-Almond Kuchen, 74
Sour Cream Kuchen, 99

INDEX

Cool Treats

Banana Split Trifle, 87
Frosty Butter Pecan Crunch Pie, 53
Isabella's Ice Cream Pie, 65
Julie's Strawberry Yum-Yum, 83
Nathaniel's Chocolate Bowl, 94
Prize Peanut Butter-Chocolate Dessert, 82

Mini Pies

Apple Hand Pies, 40
Apricot Pockets, 64
Mini Pie Bites, 61
Sweet Cherry Triangles, 71

Pies

$165 Blackberry-Apple Pie, 49
Banana Pudding Pie, 44
Berry-Rhubarb Pie, 69
Blue-Ribbon Pecan Pie, 42
Blueberry Cream Pie, 45
Caramel Apple Pie, 43
Connie's Coconut Kentucky Pie, 66
Country Harvest Pie, 55
Cranberry-Pear Streusel Pie, 50
Fabulous Sweet Potato Pie, 63
Fresh Strawberry Pie, 51

Gingersnap Pumpkin Pie, 62
Golden Tequila Lime Tart, 57
Grandma Katie's Glacé Pie, 72
Honey Pumpkin Pie, 73
Mock Apple Pie, 67
Nan's Chocolate Pie, 56
Osgood Pie, 70
Peach Melba Pie, 41
Peanut Butter Pie, 52
Raspberry Custard Pie, 58
Rustic Country Cherry Pie, 59
Rustic Pear Tart, 68
Skillet Cherry Pie, 48
Sour Cherry Lattice Pie, 47
Sour Cream Lemon Pie, 60
Tennessee Fudge Pie, 46
Upside-Down Apple-Pecan Pie, 54

Puddings

Cinnamon Bread Pudding, 100
Creamy Coconut Bread Pudding, 102
Dessert Dumplings with Caramel Sauce, 90
French Pear Pudding, 80
Honey-Custard Bread Pudding, 86
Quebec Maple Bread Pudding, 81
Rhode Island Peach Slump, 91
Virginia Apple Pudding, 101

Honey–Custard Bread Pudding, page 86

Mocha Pudding Cake, page 38

Oma's Lemon Cheesecake, page 14

Caramel Apple Pie, page 43

Our Story

Back in 1984, we were next-door neighbors raising our families in the little town of Delaware, Ohio. Two moms with small children, we were looking for a way to do what we loved and stay home with the kids too. We had always shared a love of home cooking and making memories with family & friends and so, after many a conversation over the backyard fence, **Gooseberry Patch** was born.

We put together our first catalog at our kitchen tables, enlisting the help of our loved ones wherever we could. From that very first mailing, we found an immediate connection with many of our customers and it wasn't long before we began receiving letters, photos and recipes from these new friends. In 1992, we put together our very first cookbook, compiled from hundreds of these recipes and, the rest, as they say, is history.

Hard to believe it's been over 30 years since those kitchen-table days! From that original little **Gooseberry Patch** family, we've grown to include an amazing group of creative folks who love cooking, decorating and creating as much as we do. Today, we're best known for our homestyle, family-friendly cookbooks, now recognized as national bestsellers.

JoAnn & Vickie

One thing's for sure, we couldn't have done it without our friends all across the country. Each year, we're honored to turn thousands of your recipes into our collectible cookbooks. Our hope is that each book captures the stories and heart of all of you who have shared with us. Whether you've been with us since the beginning or are just discovering us, welcome to the **Gooseberry Patch** family!

Visit us online:
www.gooseberrypatch.com
1•800•854•6673

U.S. to Metric Recipe Equivalents

Volume Measurements

1/4 teaspoon	1 mL
1/2 teaspoon	2 mL
1 teaspoon	5 mL
1 tablespoon = 3 teaspoons	15 mL
2 tablespoons = 1 fluid ounce	30 mL
1/4 cup	60 mL
1/3 cup	75 mL
1/2 cup = 4 fluid ounces	125 mL
1 cup = 8 fluid ounces	250 mL
2 cups = 1 pint =16 fluid ounces	500 mL
4 cups = 1 quart	1 L

Weights

1 ounce	30 g
4 ounces	120 g
8 ounces	225 g
16 ounces = 1 pound	450 g

Oven Temperatures

300° F	150° C
325° F	160° C
350° F	180° C
375° F	190° C
400° F	200° C
450° F	230° C

Baking Pan Sizes

Square

8x8x2 inches	2 L = 20x20x5 cm
9x9x2 inches	2.5 L = 23x23x5 cm

Rectangular

13x9x2 inches	3.5 L = 33x23x5 cm

Loaf

9x5x3 inches	2 L = 23x13x7 cm

Round

8x1-1/2 inches	1.2 L = 20x4 cm
9x1-1/2 inches	1.5 L = 23x4 cm

Recipe Abbreviations

t. = teaspoon	ltr. = liter
T. = tablespoon	oz. = ounce
c. = cup	lb. = pound
pt. = pint	doz. = dozen
qt. = quart	pkg. = package
gal. = gallon	env. = envelope

Kitchen Measurements

A pinch = 1/8 tablespoon	1 fluid ounce = 2 tablespoons
3 teaspoons = 1 tablespoon	4 fluid ounces = 1/2 cup
2 tablespoons = 1/8 cup	8 fluid ounces = 1 cup
4 tablespoons = 1/4 cup	16 fluid ounces = 1 pint
8 tablespoons = 1/2 cup	32 fluid ounces = 1 quart
16 tablespoons = 1 cup	16 ounces net weight = 1 pound
2 cups = 1 pint	
4 cups = 1 quart	
4 quarts = 1 gallon	